BILL BIRKETT

EXPLORING

40 easy circular walks

THE LAKES &

in the lake district

LOW FELLS 2

David & Charles

This book was produced in association with

www.jenningsbrewery.co.uk

The author would like to acknowledge the generous sponsorship of Jennings Brothers. Located at Cockermouth by the river Cocker, on the edge of the Lake District, Jennings have been brewing beer for over 170 years. Their real ales can be found in inns throughout the Lake District National Park. Conveniently, many of the walks in this book pass by these traditional watering holes.

TO THE LOCALS OF LAKELAND – A HARDY BREED

Photographs on page 1: (clockwise from top left) Aira Force, Walk 63; Boulder Hill, Kentmere, Walk 51; By Oak Howe, Great Langdale, Walk 45; Swans on River Bothay, Walk 43; Herdwick sheep, Walk 59; Fly agaric toadstool, Walk 75; Daffodils by River Kent, Walk 52; Bluebells, Rydal, Walk 42; Peat House, Burnmoor, Walk 63.

A DAVID & CHARLES BOOK

All photographs from the Bill Birkett Photo Library

Maps by Martin Bagness based on pre-1950 Ordnance Survey maps. Completely redrawn 2000.

First published in the UK in 2001
Reprinted in 2003
Copyright © Bill Birkett 2001

Bill Birkett has asserted his right to be identified as author of this work in accordance with the Copyright, Designs and Patents Act, 1988.

A catalogue record for this book is available from the British Library.

ISBN 0 7153 1078 X

Book design by Diana Knapp
Printed in Italy by STIGE – Turin
for David & Charles Publishers
Brunel House   Newton Abbot   Devon

CONTENTS

THE WALKS

CONTENTS   CONTENTS   CONTENTS   CONTENTS

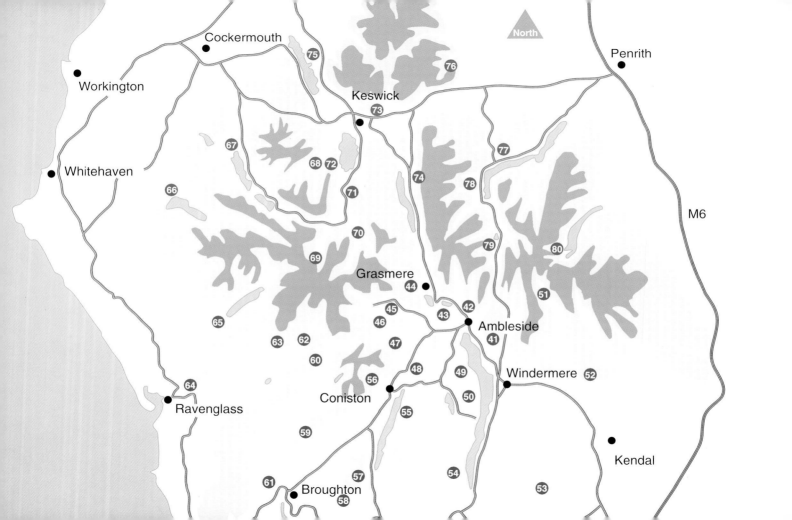

Difficulty rating: ● EASY   ● MODERATE   ● DIFFICULT

THE WALKS

41 Wansfell above Waterhead – 10km/3½ hours

42 Around the Vale of Rydal – 4km/ 1 hour

43 White Moss Common to Grasmere Lake by the River Rothay – 2.5km/1 hour

44 To Easedale Tarn – 6.5km/2½ hours

45 The Great Langdale Valley Bottom – 10km/3½ hours

46 A Circuit of Blea Tarn (with alternative – a climb to Side Pike) – 2.5km/1½ hours (3.5km/2½ hours)

47 Little Langdale's Slaters Bridge from Tilberthwaite – 6km/2½ hours

48 Tarn Hows from Glenmary Bridge (with alternative – a simple climb to Tom Heights) – 4km/1½ hours (5km/2 hours)

49 Latterbarrow Fell between Hawkshead and Windermere Lake – 6km/2 hours

50 Far to Near Sawrey – 4.5km/1½ hours

51 To the head of Kentmere – 10km/3½ hours

52 Staveley to Potter Tarn above Kentdale (with possible extention to Gurnal Dubs)– 9km/3½ hours (10.5km/4 hours)

53 Over Whitbarrow Scar rising by Chapel Head – 7km/3½ hours

54 By Finsthwaite's High Dam and Rusland Woods – 10km/3½ hours

55 A Circuit around Brantwood and above Coniston Water – 6km/2 hours

56 To Levers Water and the Coppermines Valley – 8km/2½ hours

57 To Beacon Tarn and The Beacon atop Blawith Fell – 5km/2 hours

58 Over Blawith Knott and Tottlebank Height – 6km/2½ hours

59 Rounding the East Dunnerdale Fells from Kiln Bank Cross – 6.5km/2hours

60 By the Duddon's Wallowbarrow Crag and Gorge – 6.5km/2½ hours

61 By Swinside's stone circle and Wrayslack – 8.5km/3hours

62 Upper Eskdale by Brotherilkeld – 6.5km/2¼ hours

63 By valley and fell to Eskdale's Blea Tarn – 9.5km/3½ hours

64 Over Muncaster Fell – 11km/3½ hours

65 By Wast Water Beneath the Wasdale Screes – 8km/2¾ hours

66 The round of Ennerdale Water – 11km/3 hours

67 Through Lanthwaite Wood by the foot of Crummock Water – 2.5km/1¼ hours

68 A round of the Newlands Valley – 8.5km/2½ hours

69 Seathwaite to Styhead Tarn via Taylorgill Force – 7.5km/2 hours

70 Stonethwaite to Langstrath by Twa Becks – 4km/1½ hours

71 Borrowdale's Bowderstone to Watendlath – 10km/3 hours

72 Over Cat Bells returning by Derwent Water – 7km/2½ hours

73 Keswick's Greta Gorge – 7.5km/2½ hours

74 By Thirlmere's Shore to Castle Rock – 7km/2½ hours

75 By Bassenthwaite Lake and St Bega's – 10.5km/3 hours

76 Glenderamackin and Souther Fell – 9.5km/2½ hours

77 Aira Force and High Force waterfalls – 4.5km/2 hours

78 Up Glenridding and down Glencoyne to round Sheffield Pike – 8km/2½ hours

79 A circuit of Brothers Water – 6km/1½ hours

80 Mardale Head to Castle Crag – 6.5km/2 hours

THIS PRACTICAL GUIDEBOOK is a selection of my favourite low-level walks throughout the Lake District. It is an area, for those with an eye to see and a heart to perceive, whose perfection of scale and sublime beauty – of lake, tree and fell – is oft regarded as a piece of heaven fallen to earth. Whilst many will associate my writing and photography with steep places and

Tarn Hows to Wetherlam, Walk 48

high mountains, this book is based on a lifetime's local knowledge and love of the Lake District – Britain's largest National Park. It is designed to be inspirationally attractive, whilst at the same time harmonising map, text and photograph to provide crystal-clear practical information which is suitable to be used as a guide en route.

The routes selected vary in difficulty and length from a half-hour stroll to outings of up to five-hours' duration. More typically,

they involve around two-and-a-half to three hours of leisurely walking. Sometimes level, sometimes rising to crest a low fell, mostly the walks are circular in nature, conveniently starting and finishing at the same point, providing a magnificent way to explore the many varied splendours of the area. The length and difficulty of each walk is defined in a Fact File, and within these parameters the walks are suitable for persons of average fitness and ability, young or old.

Although a number of these walks may have never previously been described in print, I make no claims for originality. Simple observation – of the stone circles and enclosures of prehistory, of Roman forts and roads underfoot, of the Celtic and Viking place names, the poetry of Wordsworth and the art of Beatrix Potter, the spoil of the miner and quarryman, the trod of the shep-

Greta Gorge, Walk 73

Over Blawith Fell, Walk 58

Beech tree, Craggy Plantation, Walk 52

herd, the work of the Ordnance Survey, of numerous Victorian and contemporary guidebooks – provide glimpses of the many who may have trod these ways. The philosophy of my route selection is simply to offer you what I feel is the best of Lakeland walking based on my own practical experience.

Despite the generally low-level nature of most of these walks there are many potential dangers to greet the unwary. Unfenced drops, open quarry holes, mineshafts, fast-flowing streams, rivers and deep lakes can all be found throughout the region. An eye should always be kept on safety and children should be carefully supervised at all times. Of course whilst one of the considerable attractions of the Lake District is the marked contrast of its four seasons, offering a variety of walking throughout the year, the walker must be adequately equipped to deal with the prevailing conditions. Similarly provision must also be made for rapidly changing weather. Wordsworth's poignant poem 'Lucy Gray' is based in fact and should be heeded:

The storm came on before its time:
She wandered up and down;
And many a hill did Lucy climb:
But never reached the town.

Summit cairn and Rowan, Blawith Knott, Walk 58

To keep the cost of this guidebook as low as possible without compromising quality, and to maintain a convenient and carryable size, the selection of walks has been limited to forty. There are currently two books available in this series: Book 1 and Book 2. Each book describes unique and different walks throughout the region. Together they form the most comprehensive and definitive walkers' guide to the lakes and low fells of the Lake District National Park. It is the author's ambition to extend coverage of the Lake District, and also to apply the same philosophy to other areas of outstanding beauty and interest.

Kentmere Church, Walk 51

Walking is a lifelong ever-changing experience. It deepens your contact with nature – the earth and wind, the sounds and smells, the sun and cold, the hard and the soft – and it quickens your observation of the infinite beauty of the natural world in harmony with man's ingenuity. In short it heightens the emotions, liberates the body, sharpens the mind and enriches the spirit. I have trod these routes many times: with my parents, alone, with friends, and currently with my young family. They are never the same; I always discover something new, and I hope to walk them in old age. Should you find such riches then I feel this guidebook will have achieved something quite remarkable.

INTRODUCTION   INTRODUCTION   INTRODUCTION

HOW TO USE THIS GUIDE

Each walk is presented on one easy-to-view double-page spread (like a sheet of writing paper – turn the book around to read it) which includes essential information to help you easily locate and select the walk, a concise route description and clear map detailing the route. Photographs illustrate the overall nature of the area and highlight particular points of interest, so capturing the overall ambience of each walk.

WALK NUMBER
See area map on page 4 for location

WALK 47 WALK 47 WALK 47 WALK 47 WALK 47

WALK NAME

LITTLE LANGDALE'S SLATERS BRIDGE FROM TILBERTHWAITE

PREVIEW
Key locations en route

High Tilberthwaite Farm, Knotts, Hall Garth, Slaters Bridge, The Ford, Moss Rigg Wood

INTRODUCTION
Gives location with respect to nearest centre and provides brief descriptive 'taster'

4KM N OF CONISTON. FROM TILBERTHWAITE A SECRETIVE WOODED VALLEY CUTS THROUGH THE HILLS, THROUGH A LANDSCAPE HEAVILY INFLUENCED BY THE EFFECTS OF SLATE QUARRYING, TO CONNECT LITTLE LANGDALE TO THE VALE OF CONISTON. TAKING THE HIGH ROAD FROM TILBERTHWAITE BEFORE DROPPING TO SLATERS BRIDGE THIS ROUTE LOOPS AROUND LITTLE LANGDALE TO RETURN BY MOSS RIGG WOODS.

STEP BY STEP
A balanced route description specifying key locations and highlighting points of particular interest. An alternative route may also be suggested

STEP BY STEP

▶ From the car park cross the little bridge to pass the hamlet of Low Tilberthwaite. Continue along the level road to High Tilberthwaite Farm. Ascend left through the gate and take the stony quarry track which winds over the Knotts offering scenic views as it leads down towards Little Langdale Tarn.

▶ At the junction of tracks turn right. The track leads to the buildings of High Hall Garth and then down the steep little hill to Low Hall Garth. Keep along the track until a kissing gate or stone stile lead through the wall and across the field to the distinctive Slaters Bridge spanning a young River Brathay. The slate bridge consists of two main spans; the first that of a stone arch and the second that of a single great slab. Said to be of Roman origin it has over the years most certainly been used by slate quarrymen from Little Langdale.

PHOTOGRAPHS
A variety of images have been chosen to span the seasons. While some are intended to capture the individual character of the walk by portraying the overall scenic splendour of the region, others do so by highlighting key points of interest

The track to Hall Garth

▶ Beyond the bridge take the path which bears off right through the (second) gap in the stone wall and follow this up through the fields to

Slaters Bridge

ROUTE MAP

KEY TO MAP SYMBOLS

	main road
	lane
	walled track — on the described walk
	unwalled track — on the described walk
	footpath — on the described walk
	walled track — not on the described walk
	unwalled track — not on the described walk
	footpath — not on the described walk
	river
	stream
	waterfall
	bridge
	lake or tarn
	contour (100')
	woodland
	built-up area
	buildings/ farm
	crag
	summit
	pub
	cafe
	youth hostel
	wall or fence (only shown where helpful for route-finding)

Little Langdale

Little Langdale Tarn

Slaters Bridge

Hall Garth

ford

quarries

quarries

Moss Rigg

Knotts

quarries

Hodge Close

High Tilberthwaite

Tilberthwaite Gill

P

start & finish

1 kilometre

N

Lane to the ford, Little Langdale

Little Langdale Tarn

a kissing gate. Descend to a further kissing gate which leads onto the surfaced road (Little Langdale village centre and the Three Shires Inn are found just off route up to the left). Go right along the road. Continue along the unsurfaced track, elevated slate parapet to the right, useful in times of flood, to cross the wooden footbridge at The Ford.

▶ Bear left and then right at the first junction. Carry on along the stone track and through the oakwoods of Moss Rigg until a further junction. Take the track which ascends to the right. Despite having the option of a firm's Landrover my father walked this way to work at Moss Rigg Quarry six days a week until he was sixty five. After that he cut down his hours! Keep straight on, a further track comes in from the right, until a final little hill reveals the buildings of High Tilberthwaite Farm beyond.

WALK 47 FACT FILE

LENGTH: 6KM
TIME: 2½ HOURS
DIFFICULTY: MODERATE, MAINLY ON GOOD TRACKS AND WITH GRADUAL ASCENT
START & FINISH: TILBERTHWAITE

QUARRY BANK CAR PARK (307 009)
MAPS: OS L90 OR OL7
ACCESS: FOLLOW THE A593 NORTH FROM CONISTON TO TURN LEFT TO TILBERTHWAITE

WATERING HOLES: NONE EN ROUTE – THREE SHIRES INN IN LITTLE LANGDALE IS NEARBY

FACT FILE This concise and easy-reference format provides essential information for planning, locating and executing the walk. LENGTH is given in kilometres. TIME is that required for a leisurely stroll whilst enjoying the sights on the way. DIFFICULTY is categorised as EASY: a straightforward non-strenuous walk; MODERATE: may include sections of ascent and descent and/or some rough going; DIFFICULT: may include strenuous ascent and descent, rough going, longevity, or require care with route-finding. NOTE: In reasonably fair summer conditions these walks are suitable for all the family and generally follow well-defined tracks or paths. This section may also include a note on potential dangers such as unfenced cliffs. START & FINISH The walks are mostly circular and start and finish at the same point with a map reference provided. MAPS: Reference is made to the Ordinance Survey Landranger (1:50,000 scale) and Outdoor Leisure (1:25, 000 scale). ACCESS is described from the nearest centre. WATERING HOLES Places for refreshment en route or those located nearby.

HOW TO USE THIS GUIDE HOW TO USE THIS GUIDE

May bluebells in Rydal Woods, Walk 42

THE LAKE DISTRICT NATIONAL PARK is the largest in Britain, with an area of some 2,242sq km. Located at the north-west extremity of England, with the Solway Firth to the north and Scotland beyond, it is roughly circular in plan. Its 55km diameter stretches from Ravenglass on the west coast to Shap Abbey in the east, from Caldbeck in the north to Lindale and Morecambe

Taylorgill Force, Walk 69

Bay in the south. Its physical landscape is that of a mountain region, whose formative geological activity started some 500 million years ago, subsequently and dramatically shaped by the effects of glaciation.

During the last ice age, some 15,000 years ago, the movement of huge thicknesses of ice carved out a system of valleys which, roughly speaking, radiate out from the central high point of Scafell Pike, at 978m the highest mountain in England. Often likened to the spokes of a wheel these deep,

narrow valleys, with their lakes, shape and define six distinctly different areas of mountains (see Complete Lakeland Fells by the author for details). The individual hills are known as fells, from the Viking fjall. From its high fells to deep valleys, by its cascading becks and great lakes, by woods, fields and craggy steeps, it is an area of immense beauty, great diversity and striking contrast.

The geology of the region is remarkably varied, and it is the rocks whose properties, soils and

mineralisation have most influenced the subsequent shaping of the landscape at the hands of man. In brief, some 450 million years ago the oldest rocks of the region were

Prehistoric settlement boulders, Dovedale, Walk 79

Over Beacon Tarn to Coniston Fells, Walk 57

Great Langdale valley bottom, pikes above, Walk 45

River Duddon, Wallowbarrow Gorge, Walk 60

Over Derwent Water to Skiddaw, Walk 71

laid as sedimentary deposits; these are the Skiddaw slates which mainly shape the northern fells. Next followed a period of intense volcanic activity, uplift and mineralisation which produced the core of the region – these hard rocks are known as the Borrowdale volcanics, which typically form the Langdale Pikes. The volcanics are underlain by granite, that of Eskdale and Ennerdale. Around 420 million years ago another period of flooding produced the sedimentary Silurian slates, and these softer rocks form the

Autumn, Stockghyll Lane, Ambleside, Walk 41

gentler, more rounded landscape of Windermere Lake and Coniston Water. The white fossilised sedimentary limestones found on the southern periphery, those of Scout Scar and Whitbarrow Scar, date from the Carboniferous period of some 300 million years ago.

To this geological skeleton add a rich botanical flora, a fine mixture of deciduous trees, and wildlife: deer, squirrel, fox, golden eagle and peregrine falcon. Apply the industrious hand of man, his farms, mines and inns, his art and ingenuity, and you have a unique and fascinating landscape. Man first began to farm the landscape circa 5,000 BC during the Neolithic period. Using stone axes manufactured from the fine-grained volcanic tuff found most notably on the Langdale Pikes, he felled the trees to clear the valleys. Recently recorded, though known and photographed by the author for many years, Neolithic man left his art in the form of rock drawings on a

Swinside Stone Circle, Walk 61

number of valley boulders. Most dramatically, the stone circles of Castlerigg and Swinside were also constructed during this period. Later came the Bronze Age, circa 3,000 BC, and presumably the first copper mines of the Coniston fells.

The Romans, who had a profound influence on the area, arrived circa 80 AD and didn't depart until early 400 AD. The most dramatic evidence of their occupation remains in the form of Hardknott Fort above Eskdale, Walls Castle (the

The resurgence at Beck Head, Walk 53

highest free-standing Roman building in northern England) and the Roman roads over the great ridge of High Street and Muncaster Fell. Somewhere around 900 AD the Vikings arrived and it is they who have probably done the most to influence the existing shape of the region. Principally farmers, it was they who named the fells and many features of the landscape. In fact we remain to this day – Birkett is of Norse origin, and my grandfather used to speak a language, which went beyond dialect, directly akin to old Norse. He found it very useful when the vicar called and failed to understand a single word! (True story.)

Two huge influences on the landscape were mineral mining, chiefly for copper and lead, and slate quarrying. Whilst mining is certainly an activity of pre-history, written record shows that the monks of Furness, circa 1150, mined haematite and manufactured iron in bloomeries sited throughout the region. Incidentally they kept their records in pencil using graphite from

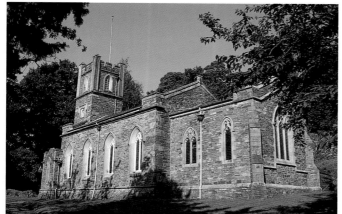

Rydal Church by Dora's Field, Walk 41

Seathwaite (then the only world source of the material). Reputedly the Romans worked slate, though slate quarrying increased dramatically during the industrial revolution, a period of growth which made huge demands for roofing material.

The first tourist guidebook is reputed to be that of Father West in 1778, and the appreciation of the beauty of the Lake District took off in earnest from then on. The Romantic poets of the early 1800s consolidated the position, notably under the influence of William Wordsworth, who also produced a best-selling guidebook to the area. Later, twentieth-century influences included Beatrix Potter with her 'Peter Rabbit' books and Hugh Walpole's 'Rogue Herries' novels.

The Lake District officially became a National Park in the 1950s. Today a number of organised bodies have the region's best interests at heart. These of course include the National Park Authority and the National Trust, both of whom are ably assisted by energetic bands of volunteers who generously give their time to support the professionals. Other protective organisations include the Friends of the Lake District and the Cumbria Broadleaves partnership.

One of the great joys of the Lake District is its freedom of access. Above the fell wall this is generally unrestricted, and below in the dales and through the fields there exists a comprehensive system

Bill Birkett

of rights of way – fully utilised by this book. Whatever the weather, throughout the seasons the Lake District's stone-built farms and cottages, wild fells, enchanting woods, dashing waterfalls, lakes and tarns and welcoming inns present an ever-changing kaleidoscope of mood and colour. It really is one of the most special places on earth.

By Ennerdale Water, Walk 66

Sunset over Ennerdale Water, Walk 66

LAKELAND▲LAKELAND IN A NUTSHELL ▲LAKELAND

WANSFELL ABOVE WATERHEAD

Wansfell Pike, The Hundreds, Nanny Lane, Troutbeck, Robin Lane, Skelghyll Wood, Jenkin Crag

INTRODUCTION

AMBLESIDE. AT THE HEAD OF WINDERMERE LAKE, DEFINED BY THE KIRKSTONE ROAD TO THE WEST AND TROUTBECK TO THE EAST, GENTLE WANSFELL WATCHES OVER THE LITTLE TOWN OF AMBLESIDE. THIS CLOCKWISE CIRCUIT LEADS STEEPLY OVER WANSFELL PIKE BEFORE DESCENDING TO TROUTBECK AND MAKING RETURN BY A LOW TRAVERSE OVERLOOKING WINDERMERE LAKE.

Wansfell above the Serpentine, near Waterhead

STEP BY STEP

▶ Behind Ambleside's Market Hall, Cheapside rises to Stockghyll Lane. Ascend the surfaced lane (passing Stockgyhll Force thundering unseen in the woods to the left) until with the old Kelsick Grammar School to the right (on games day – Wednesdays – we climbed this hill twice) the track passes through a gate and becomes unsurfaced. In a little way an iron ladder stile ascends to the right and leads to a path rising to a further ladder stile over a stone wall. The path steepens through the small oaks to climb directly up the flanks of Wansfell Pike. Keep left at the craggy top to crest the high rock knoll. The view over Windermere Lake and to the high fells all around cannot fail to take your breath away – however many times you may have seen it.

▶ Cross the stile and bear left descending the worn path over The Hundreds to join the walled lane of Nanny Lane leading to the Troutbeck Road. The way goes right although a short detour to the left leads to The Mortal Man whose sign may bring a smile;

"Oh mortal man that lives by bread,
What is it makes thy nose so red?
Thou silly fool that looks so pale,
'Tis drinking Sally Birketts ale."

The ascent to Wansfell Pike

Back on route a number of wells issue above the road, including Margarets, James and St John's, before the post office building stands to the right. Bear right up the track of Robin Lane. The last stone cottage is inscribed 'BB 1732'. Continue to follow the lane it begins to rise. Here the way leads off to the left (signed Ambleside).

The path/track leads over Hol Beck before rising briefly to pass High Skelghyll and on to enter Skelghyll Wood. A gap in the wall (and sign) lead to Jenkin Crag. This once popular Victorian view point offers an astonishing view out over Windermere Lake even though the trees now partly obscure the vista. Return to the track which descends gradually to Ambleside to gain the main road opposite Hayes Garden Centre.

Map labels

P start & finish

Stockghyll Force
Stockghyll Lane

AMBLESIDE

Wansfell Pike

Nanny Lane

The Hundreds

Water-head

The Mortal Man

Troutbeck

High Skelghyll

Lake Windermere

A591

Jenkin Crag

Post Office

N

1 kilometre

Robin Lane

Lake Windermere from Wansfell Pike

WALK 41 FACT FILE

LENGTH: 10KM
TIME: 3½ HOURS
DIFFICULTY: DIFFICULT; WITH STRENUOUS ASCENT
START & FINISH: MARKET HALL, CENTRAL AMBLESIDE (377 045)
MAPS: OS L90 OR OL7
ACCESS: AMBLESIDE'S MAIN CAR PARK IS LOCATED BY THE A591 RYDAL ROAD TO KESWICK
WATERING HOLES: PLENTIFUL IN AMBLESIDE, EN ROUTE ARE THE MORTAL MAN INN AND TROUTBECK POST OFFICE TEA ROOM

AROUND THE VALE OF RYDAL

Cote How, Rydal Church, Dora's Field, Rydal Hall, Rydal Park, Scandale Bridge, Rydal Steps

2KM N OF AMBLESIDE. BETWEEN AMBLESIDE AND GRASMERE, NESTLING BENEATH HIGH FELLS AT THE FOOT OF RYDAL WATER, THE HAMLET OF RYDAL IS FAMOUS BOTH FOR CONNECTIONS WITH WORDSWORTH AND ITS PICTURESQUE CHARM. THIS ROUND EXPLORES DORA'S FIELD AND NUMEROUS POINTS OF INTEREST SITED AROUND THE HAMLET.

STEP BY STEP

▶ Rydal Mount was the home of William Wordsworth between 1813 and 1850. This walk passes just below the house after making an exploration of Dora's Field, Wordsworth's gift to his favourite daughter, noted for its wonderful display of golden daffodils which bloom in April.

▶ From the car park go left to climb the road until, opposite Cote How Cottages, a kissing gate on the right leads to steps down through Steps End Wood. Beyond the wood the path leads down rightwards over the field to the footbridge crossing the River Rothay. Join the road and bear right until a road ascends to the left. Follow this to the Rydal Church. Enter the gate and pass through the churchyard to find a gate leading into Dora's Field. A clockwise round, following the path and steps around the wooded hillside, is recommended before returning to the church.

▶ Exit left onto the road (Rydal Mount lies a little higher) and then take the lane to the right to pass behind the back of Rydal Hall. The track leads between the buildings associated with the hall, over a bridge and on rightwards, through the rhododendrons and

Daffodils on Dora's Field

In May the Rydal Woods are full of bluebells

exotic trees of Rydal Park. Continue along the lane. In season Rydal Sheep Dog Trials and Ambleside Show are held in the fields to the right. Exit through great iron gates onto the A591 by Scandale Bridge

▶ Cross the road and go right, on the pavement, to follow by the invariably busy A591 for 500 metres until a kissing gate (signed) gives access to the field on the left just beyond a tree-clad knoll (beyond the cricket field). There is no obvious path across the field (at the time of writing) – take a line bearing diagonally right to a levelling in the shoulder of the hill opposite and continue, passing right of a cluster of oaks, to intercept the stepping stones of Rydal Steps situated at the far corner of the field. Cross the River Rothay, impossible in times of heavy rain, and go right along the road to bear left by Pelter Bridge back to the car park.

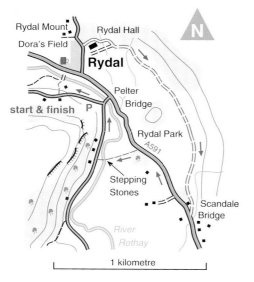

Rydal village

Above: Rydal steps over River Rothay

Left: Rydal Hall as the colours turn

WALK 42 FACT FILE

LENGTH: 4KM
TIME: 1 HOUR
DIFFICULTY: EASY
START & FINISH: PELTER BRIDGE CAR PARK (364 060)

MAPS: OS L90 OR OL7
ACCESS: FOLLOW THE A591 NORTH FROM AMBLESIDE UNTIL JUST BEFORE ENTERING THE HAMLET OF RYDAL, PELTER BRIDGE LIES TO THE LEFT. GO OVER THE BRIDGE AND IMMEDIATELY RIGHT TO THE CAR PARK

WATERING HOLES: BADGER BAR OPPOSITE STEPS END FOOTBRIDGE EN ROUTE

WHITE MOSS COMMON TO GRASMERE LAKE BY THE RIVER ROTHAY

White Moss Common, River Rothay, Baneriggs Wood, Grasmere Lake, Loughrigg Wood

INTRODUCTION

4KM NW OF AMBLESIDE. FROM THE BOTTOM OF GRASMERE LAKE THE RIVER ROTHAY SQUEEZES BETWEEN HIGH FELLS, FLOWS EAST THROUGH SYLVAN DALE AND BY WHITE MOSS COMMON, BEFORE PONDING ONCE AGAIN TO FORM RYDAL WATER. THIS WALK FOLLOWS THE NORTH BANK OF THE RIVER CROSSING TO THE BOTTOM OF THE LAKE AND RETURNING ALONG THE OPPOSITE BANK.

STEP BY STEP

Often it's the simplest things in life that provide the most pleasure; a single snowflake drifting from a wintry sky, a ray of sunshine piercing grey cloud. So it is with this short, lovely walk to Grasmere Lake. Beginning from the lower car park avoids having to make a crossing of the road. Leave the back of the car park to follow the track, over a small footbridge, to the bend in the river. A favourite swimming/paddling area in summer, much frequented by swans and ducks looking for titbits. Continue to wooden footbridge, supported on stone pillars, which crosses the River Rothay. Don't

Footbridge at White Moss Common

cross but take the gate on the right by the bridge and follow the track along the field edge. Gain Baneriggs Woods and rise through the magnificent oaks. Slight descent leads to a footbridge, and a crossing made of the River Rothay.

Hawthorn and bluebells by south shore, Grasmere Lake

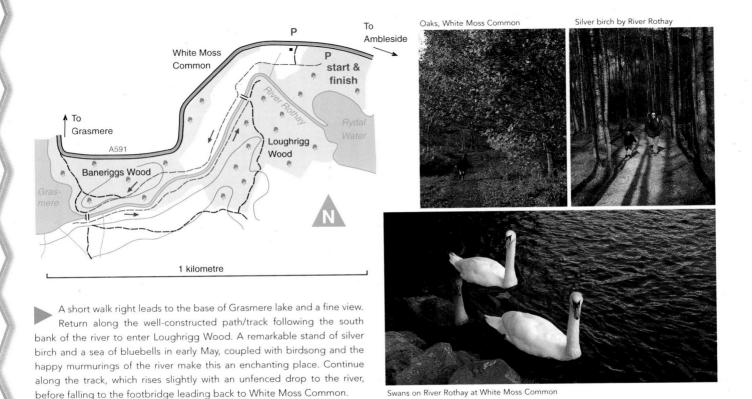

Oaks, White Moss Common

Silver birch by River Rothay

Swans on River Rothay at White Moss Common

A short walk right leads to the base of Grasmere lake and a fine view. Return along the well-constructed path/track following the south bank of the river to enter Loughrigg Wood. A remarkable stand of silver birch and a sea of bluebells in early May, coupled with birdsong and the happy murmurings of the river make this an enchanting place. Continue along the track, which rises slightly with an unfenced drop to the river, before falling to the footbridge leading back to White Moss Common.

WALK 43 FACT FILE

LENGTH: 2.5KM
TIME: 1 HOUR
DIFFICULTY: EASY (VERY)
START & FINISH: WHITE MOSS COMMON LOWER CAR PARK (349 065)

MAPS: OS L90 OR OL7
ACCESS: LEAVE AMBLESIDE ON THE A591 IN THE DIRECTION OF GRASMERE TO FIND WHITE MOSS COMMON IN 3KM. NATIONAL TRUST CAR PARKS LOCATED

ABOVE AND BELOW THE ROAD
WATERING HOLES: FRED PERRUZA ICE CREAM VAN BY UPPER CAR PARK

TO EASEDALE TARN

Goody Bridge, Brimmer Head Farm, Sourmilk Gill, Easedale Tarn, Far Easedale, Stythwaite Steps

GRASMERE. SITED QUIETLY ABOVE THE BUSTLE OF GRASMERE VILLAGE, THE WOODS, MEADOWS, AND PURPLE STAINED STONE COTTAGES OF TRANQUIL EASEDALE LEAD TO THE WILDER MOUNTAIN ENVIRONMENTS OF THE CELEBRATED EASEDALE TARN AND FAR EASEDALE. ASCENDING TO EASEDALE BY THE TUMBLING WATERFALLS OF SOURMILK GILL THIS ROUTE THEN MAKES DESCENT INTO FAR EASEDALE.

The mountain sanctuary of Easedale Tarn

STEP BY STEP

▶ Across the road from the car park a permissive path leads alongside the road before joining it below Goody Bridge. Continue up the road until it levels. A wooden footbridge and an ancient ford, followed by a stone slab, lead left into the trees. Keep along the cobbled path, following the tree-clad bank of the beck, to pass the stone arch of New Bridge. With the buildings of Brimmer Head Farm over to the right, the path begins to ascend by the side of a stone wall. Having gained open fellside, the well-defined path swings back right to intercept the delightful waterfalls of Sourmilk Gill.

▶ Beyond the falls the going eases before a final pull leads to a large boulder and the stone remains of a Victorian Tea House which once overlooked Easedale Tarn. Located in a wonderfully wild mountain setting, watched over by the steeps of Tarn Crag, two basins of dark water merge to take the shape of a figure-of-eight fish. Whilst head and body are chiefly surrounded by beach and open ground, the tail nestles amidst a jumble of fallen boulders and heaped morraine. This is one of Lakeland's most intriguing high mountain tarns. Cross the outflow by the stepping stones and follow the

Sourmilk Gill

path which runs to the north of Sourmilk Gill, beneath a craggy outcrop, past clusters of boulders, to cross the watershed and make a simple descent into Far Easedale.

▶ Cross Far Easedale Gill beck by the footbridge, or take the Stythwaite Steps stepping stones, to bear right and enter a stone-walled lane. This delightful stony track, with fields to the right and craggy

Stepping stones below the tarn

Boulder and ex-tea house by Easedale Tarn

outcrops to the left, passes by an old farmstead with stone door lintel inscribed 'ESP 1738', and finally leads to a small wood. Continue through a gate, descending to the right to pass between the fine houses of the upper hamlet of Easedale. Follow the road through the hay meadow, to a gate regaining the point where the old ford and footbridge cross Easedale Beck.

Map labels:
Far Easedale
Stythwaite Steps
N
Easedale Tarn
Sour Milk Gill
falls
Brimmer Head
Thorny How
Goody Bridge start & finish
P
To Grasmere
1 kilometre

WALK 44 FACT FILE

LENGTH: 6.5KM
TIME: 2½ HOURS
DIFFICULTY: EASY TO MODERATE, WITH STRAIGHTFORWARD ASCENT AND DESCENT
START & FINISH: CAR PARK BY THE EASEDALE ROAD ABOVE GRASMERE (334 080)

MAPS: OS L90 OR OL7
ACCESS: GRASMERE CAN BE FOUND NORTH OF AMBLESIDE SOME 6KM ALONG THE A591 TOWARDS KESWICK. ASCEND THE EASEDALE ROAD FROM THE CENTRE OF GRASMERE FOR 0.5KM

WATERING HOLES: ICE CREAMS AT HEAD OF ROAD EN ROUTE, EXTENSIVE RANGE WITHIN GRASMERE BELOW

THE GREAT LANGDALE VALLEY BOTTOM

Side House Farm, Oak Howe Farm, Baysbrown Farm, Elterwater, Chapel Stile, Thrang Farm

INTRODUCTION

10.5KM W OF AMBLESIDE. DOMINATED BY THE HIGH LANGDALE PIKES, GREAT LANGDALE, WITH ITS TWO VILLAGES OF ELTERWATER AND CHAPEL STILE AND ITS SMATTERING OF SMALL FARMS, HAS LONG BEEN ONE OF THE MOST CELEBRATED MOUNTAIN VALLEYS IN GREAT BRITAIN. SAVOURING THE ATMOSPHERE OF THIS REMARKABLE DALE THIS WALK MAKES AN ANTICLOCKWISE CIRCUIT AROUND THE VALLEY BOTTOM.

STEP BY STEP

From the large car park bear right (west) up the road for a short way until a gate on the left opens to the track which leads to Side House Farm. Pass the farm and go left, following the path across the open hillside. After intercepting a narrow stone lane the route follows along and then between stone walls to a barn by Oak Howe Farm (Oak How Needle stands on the fellside above).

Go right at the junction (away from the farm) and follow the track to Baysbrown Farm. Pass the farm, taking the surfaced road through the oaks and mixed deciduous Baysbrown Wood. Keep straight on, passing Crossgates House, following the surfaced road. Eventually this falls, after being intercepted by the stony track of Ullets Nest, to Elterwater. Turn left. The village lies just beyond the bridge over Great Langdale Beck. This route, however, bears left up the track/road which leads off just before the bridge is crossed.

Follow the road until steps lead down and right, to the banks of the river. Follow the path until the river is crossed by a wooden footbridge. Bear left along the road, passing Wainwrights Inn, until opposite Chapel

Footbridge crossing Langdale Beck

Over the cottages of Chapel Stile with Bowfell and Langdale Pikes beyond

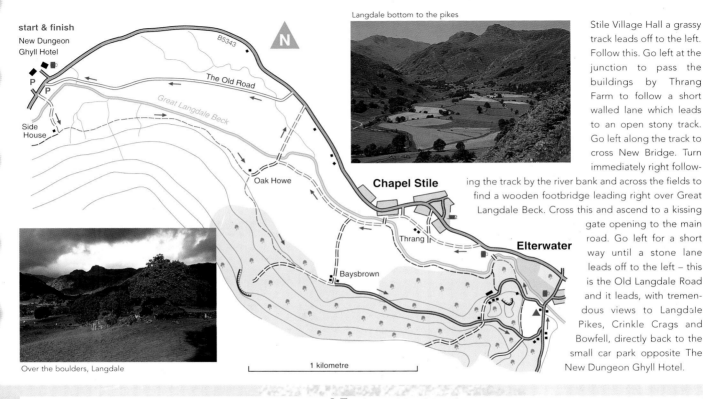

start & finish
New Dungeon Ghyll Hotel

P

Side House

B5343

N

The Old Road

Great Langdale Beck

Oak Howe

Langdale bottom to the pikes

Chapel Stile

Thrang

Baysbrown

Elterwater

1 kilometre

Over the boulders, Langdale

Stile Village Hall a grassy track leads off to the left. Follow this. Go left at the junction to pass the buildings by Thrang Farm to follow a short walled lane which leads to an open stony track. Go left along the track to cross New Bridge. Turn immediately right following the track by the river bank and across the fields to find a wooden footbridge leading right over Great Langdale Beck. Cross this and ascend to a kissing gate opening to the main road. Go left for a short way until a stone lane leads off to the left – this is the Old Langdale Road and it leads, with tremendous views to Langdale Pikes, Crinkle Crags and Bowfell, directly back to the small car park opposite The New Dungeon Ghyll Hotel.

WALK 45 FACT FILE

LENGTH: 10KM
TIME: 3½ HOURS
DIFFICULTY: EASY
START & FINISH: CAR PARKS NEAR NEW DUNGEON GHYLL HOTEL (295 064)
MAPS: OS L90 OR OL6 & OL7

ACCESS: LEAVE AMBLESIDE ON THE A593 IN THE DIRECTION OF CONISTON TO REACH SKELWITH BRIDGE IN 4KM. TURN RIGHT FOLLOWING THE GREAT LANGDALE ROAD TO PASS THE NEW DUNGEON GHYLL HOTEL. SMALL CAR PARK OPPOSITE HOTEL

ENTRANCE OR EXTENSIVE CAR PARK ON RIGHT
WATERING HOLES: STICKLE BARN, BRITTANIA INN AT ELTERWATER, WAINWRIGHTS INN AND A CAFE AT CHAPEL STILE

A CIRCUIT OF BLEA TARN (WITH ALTERNATIVE – A CLIMB TO SIDE PIKE)

Blea Tarn, Blea Tarn Plantation, Blea Tarn Pass, (Side Pike), Bleatarn House, Echo Stone

14KM W OF AMBLESIDE. WITH ONE SOLITARY FARM AND OVERLOOKED BY SIDE PIKE, THE SUBLIME BLEA TARN RESTS IN SPLENDID ISOLATION SUSPENDED BETWEEN THE TWO LANGDALES, LITTLE AND GREAT. THIS WALK MAKES A SIMPLE CLOCKWISE PERAMBULATION WITH THE ALTERNATIVE INCLUSION OF AN ASCENT OF THE ROCKY SPIRE OF SIDE PIKE.

To Langdale Pikes from Blea Tarn

STEP BY STEP

Little Blea Tarn has many moods and this is a walk for all seasons. Although recent operations have thinned them out, in late April or May the rhododendrons in Blea Tarn Plantation can offer a wonderful display of reddy pink to contrast with the green of the Scots Pine and mixed conifers. Take the gate on the opposite side of the road to the car park and follow the level path to enter the trees. Cross the little wooden footbridge over the issuing stream. Go right. At a point where the main footpath bears left away from the edge of the tarn, it is worth walking right to the rocky point and its stand of Scots Pine. Return to

To Blea Tarn Plantation

the main path and follow it to leave the woods. Continue along the rough path which rises slowly before contouring easily to the cattle grid at the head of the Blea Tarn Pass.

The alternative route climbing Side Pike takes the stile on the opposite side of the road before first bearing left, then ascending back right to climb the shoulder of the pike on a well-defined path. Continue to the rocky summit knoll with its staggering views across the head of Great Langdale to the Langdale Pikes, Bowfell and Crinkle Crags. Take care for steep cliffs lie directly below the summit cone – there is no safe passage straight on. Descend for a short way by the same path taken in ascent, until a smaller path breaks off to the left. This descends slightly then contours left beneath the rocky Blea tarn face of the pike to find a narrow rift between a great flake of rock and the face of the crag – The Squeeze Flake.

Pass through this, difficulty dependent on girth, to follow the path descending to a little stile over the wire fence. Steep descent leads to the road. The regular route bears right to follow the road. Pass beneath the bent larch by Bleatarn House and note the boulder just before the car park – locals know this as the Echo Stone.

To Great Langdale

Side Pike

alternative route to Side Pike

cattle grid

Bleatarn House

Blea Tarn

Echo Stone

P

start & finish

To Little Langdale

N

1 kilometre

Bleatarn House

Autumn colours at Blea Tarn

WALK 46 FACT FILE

LENGTH: 2½KM (3.5KM WITH ALT)
TIME: 1.5 HOURS (2.5 HOURS WITH ALT)
DIFFICULTY: EASY (DIFFICULT WITH ALT)

START & FINISH: BLEA TARN CAR PARK (296 043)
MAPS: OS L90 OR OL7
ACCESS: CAN BE REACHED FROM EITHER

THE LITTLE OR GREAT LANGDALE VALLEYS
WATERING HOLES: NONE EN ROUTE – NEAREST ARE OLD DUNGEON GHYLL HOTEL IN GL, THREE SHIRES INN IN LL

LITTLE LANGDALE'S SLATERS BRIDGE FROM TILBERTHWAITE

High Tilberthwaite Farm, Knotts, Hall Garth, Slaters Bridge, The Ford, Moss Rigg Wood

INTRODUCTION

4KM N OF CONISTON. FROM TILBERTHWAITE A SECRETIVE WOODED VALLEY CUTS THROUGH THE HILLS, THROUGH A LANDSCAPE HEAVILY INFLUENCED BY THE EFFECTS OF SLATE QUARRYING, TO CONNECT LITTLE LANGDALE TO THE VALE OF CONISTON. TAKING THE HIGH ROAD FROM TILBERTHWAITE BEFORE DROPPING TO SLATERS BRIDGE THIS ROUTE LOOPS AROUND LITTLE LANGDALE TO RETURN BY MOSS RIGG WOODS.

STEP BY STEP

From the car park cross the little bridge to pass the hamlet of Low Tilberthwaite. Continue along the level road to High Tilberthwaite Farm. Ascend left through the gate and take the stony quarry track which winds over the Knotts offering scenic views as it leads down towards Little Langdale Tarn.

At the junction of tracks turn right. The track leads to the buildings of High Hall Garth and then down the steep little hill to Low Hall Garth. Keep along the track until a kissing gate or stone stile lead through the wall and across the field to the distinctive Slaters Bridge spanning a young River Brathay. The slate bridge consists of two main spans; the first that of a stone arch and the second that of a single great slab. Said to be of Roman origin it has over the years most certainly been used by slate quarrymen from Little Langdale.

The track to Hall Garth

Beyond the bridge take the path which bears off right through the (second) gap in the stone wall and follow this up through the fields to

Slaters Bridge

Little Langdale

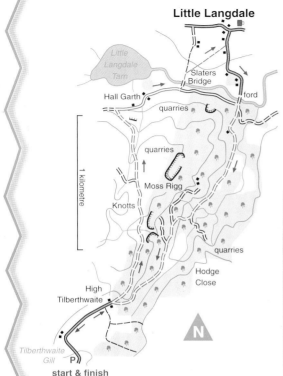

Little Langdale Tarn

Slaters Bridge

Hall Garth

quarries

ford

quarries

Moss Rigg

Knotts

quarries

Hodge Close

High Tilberthwaite

Tilberthwaite Gill

P

start & finish

1 kilometre

N

Lane to the ford, Little Langdale

Little Langdale Tarn

a kissing gate. Descend to a further kissing gate which leads onto the surfaced road (Little Langdale village centre and the Three Shires Inn are found just off route up to the left). Go right along the road. Continue along the unsurfaced track, elevated slate parapet to the right, useful in times of flood, to cross the wooden footbridge at The Ford.

▶ Bear left and then right at the first junction. Carry on along the stone track and through the oakwoods of Moss Rigg until a further junction. Take the track which ascends to the right. Despite having the option of a firm's Landrover my father walked this way to work at Moss Rigg Quarry six days a week until he was sixty five. After that he cut down his hours! Keep straight on, a further track comes in from the right, until a final little hill reveals the buildings of High Tilberthwaite Farm beyond.

WALK 47 FACT FILE

LENGTH: 6KM

TIME: 2½ HOURS

DIFFICULTY: MODERATE, MAINLY ON GOOD TRACKS AND WITH GRADUAL ASCENT

START & FINISH: TILBERTHWAITE

QUARRY BANK CAR PARK (307 009)

MAPS: OS L90 OR OL7

ACCESS: FOLLOW THE A593 NORTH FROM CONISTON TO TURN LEFT TO TILBERTHWAITE

WATERING HOLES: NONE EN ROUTE – THREE SHIRES INN IN LITTLE LANGDALE IS NEARBY

TARN HOWS FROM GLENMARY BRIDGE
(WITH ALTERNATIVE – A SIMPLE CLIMB TO TOM HEIGHTS)

Lane Head Coppice, Tarn Hows, Tom Heights Intake Plantation, Rose Castle Plantation

INTRODUCTION

3.5KM N OF CONISTON. OCCUPYING A HOLLOW IN TOM HEIGHTS, WITH A GLORIOUS BACKDROP OF HIGH LAKELAND FELLS, TARN HOWS IS PERHAPS THE MOST POPULAR BEAUTY SPOT IN THE WHOLE OF THE LAKE DISTRICT. THIS CLOCKWISE ROUND FIRST ASCENDS THROUGH WOODS TO GAIN THE TARN THEN OFFERS AN ALTERNATIVE WHICH CLIMBS TO THE SUMMIT OF TOM HEIGHTS.

STEP BY STEP

▶ Take the footbridge which crosses the beck and follow the path to rise through the mixed oakwoods of Lane Head Coppice. Arrive at Tarn Hows by the little dam and point of issue of the stream. En route a number of distinct circular flat areas represent ancient charcoal burning sites. The tarn and its island provide a heady display of mixed woods, particularly fine Scots Pine, and rhododendron. Turn left along the track and follow it in clockwise mode.

▶ Just beyond the point at which the track rises and moves away from the tarn shore to enter Tom Heights Intake Plantation, a little grassy path leads off steeply up the hillside to the left. An

Larch tree above the tarn

alternative to simple circumnavigation of the tarn, is to follow this path up to the shoulder of Tom Heights then bear right – north – along the undulating craggy crest to gain the summit cairn. The views to Wetherlam, The Langdale Pikes, Helvellyn and Fairfield are stupendous. Continue north following the shoulder in descent until a rather boggy path leads down right, winding its way through bracken, juniper and little crags to gain a

Over Tarn Hows and Tom Heights with Langdale Pikes beyond

track. Bear right to intercept the track which circumnavigates the tarn and go left along this. Add about half an hour for this extension.

▶ If the regular route is to be followed, continue along the main track bearing right at the junction of tracks to cross the little stream at the head of the tarn by a little footbridge. Continue along the track through Rose Castle Plantation, bearing right at a junction, to round the tarn with increasingly fine views to the fells beyond. Finally descend to arrive back at the dam. Locals still call Tarn Hows, 'Three Tarns' – testimony to its undammed state. As one sheet of water it retains a fascinating complexity, with its many promontories, inlets and islands. This, coupled with the lovely mixed woods, and magnificent position, make Tarn Hows a uniquely special place.

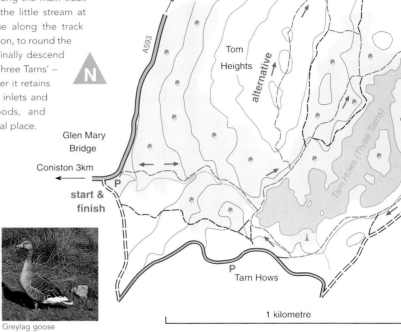

View from Tom Heights

Greylag goose

WALK 48 FACT FILE

LENGTH: 4KM (5KM WITH ALT)
TIME: 1½ HOURS (2 HOURS WITH ALT)
DIFFICULTY: EASY, WITH A SHORT ASCENT AND DESCENT (MODERATE WITH ALT)

START & FINISH: : PARKING IN THE WOODS BY GLENMARY BRIDGE SOUTH OF THE A593 (321 998)
MAPS: OS L90 & L96 OR OL7
ACCESS: FOLLOW THE A593 NORTH

FROM CONISTON TO PARK ON THE RIGHT BEFORE THE BRIDGE AND PRIOR TO REACHING YEW TREE TARN
WATERING HOLES: NONE EN ROUTE, PLENTIFOLD IN CONISTON

LATTERBARROW FELL BETWEEN HAWKSHEAD AND WINDERMERE LAKE

Scar Lane, Loanthwaite Lane, Latterbarrow, Old Intake, Rough Hows, Colthouse Hamlet

I N T R O D U C T I O N

8KM SW OF AMBLESIDE. LATTERBARROW FELL
STANDS WITH WONDERFUL OPEN ASPECT BETWEEN
THE VALE OF HAWKSHEAD AND WINDERMERE LAKE.
THIS ROUTE CLIMBS TO THE SUMMIT OF THE HILL
BEFORE TRAVERSING ITS AFFORESTED SOUTHERN
SHOULDER AND INTERCEPTING AN ANCIENT
BRIDLEWAY WHICH LEADS PLEASANTLY DOWN
TO THE HAMLET OF COLTHOUSE.

I N T R O D U C T I O N

STEP BY STEP

▶ Walk from the car park in a direction away from the village to cross the road and turn left. Pass the campsite entrance and continue to take the footpath on the right (signed) which passes the police station. Cross the fields, often muddy, and tiny footbridge, and continue to gain Scar House Lane. Go left, then almost immediately right, following the path across the field to the surfaced road of Loanthwaite Lane.

▶ Turn right ascending to a junction. Turn left to find, in 100m, a track which leads up right to Latterbarrow. Through the trees a path bears off left to make steep open ascent of the hill before continuing more easily to the masonry tower which marks the summit. The best uninterrupted views over the lake will be found a little forward of this. The great fell of Red Screes, above Ambleside, takes on tremendous proportion from this aspect.

Take the path along the shoulder in a south westerly direction to enter the conifers. The path bears first left and then right to round the top of Old Intake. Intercept the line of an old stone wall and follow it rightwards. This leads to a gate and the stony track of the ancient bridleway.

To Latterbarrow Monument

View over the head of Windermere Lake from Latterbarrow

30

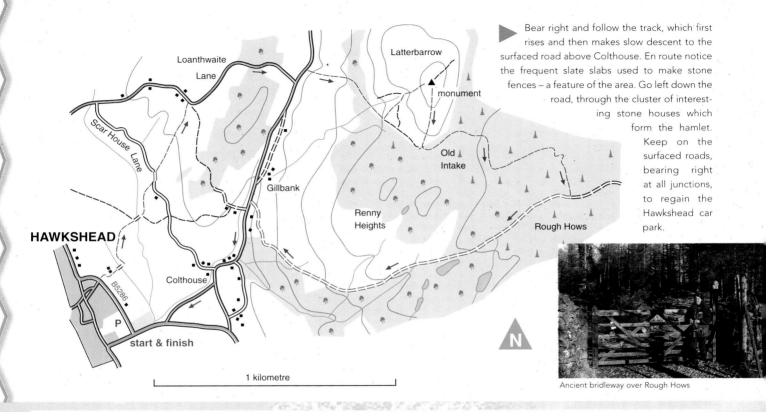

Loanthwaite
Lane

Latterbarrow

▲ monument

Scar House Lane

Gillbank

Old
Intake

HAWKSHEAD

Renny
Heights

Rough Hows

B5286

Colthouse

P

start & finish

1 kilometre

N

Bear right and follow the track, which first rises and then makes slow descent to the surfaced road above Colthouse. En route notice the frequent slate slabs used to make stone fences – a feature of the area. Go left down the road, through the cluster of interesting stone houses which form the hamlet. Keep on the surfaced roads, bearing right at all junctions, to regain the Hawkshead car park.

Ancient bridleway over Rough Hows

WALK 49 FACT FILE

LENGTH: 6KM
TIME: 2 HOURS
DIFFICULTY: MODERATE, WITH A SHORT BUT STRENUOUS ASCENT
START & FINISH: HAWKSHEAD CAR

PARK (355 981)
MAPS: OS L89 OR OL7
ACCESS: FROM AMBLESIDE FOLLOW THE A593 CONISTON ROAD TO TURN LEFT AT CLAPPERSGATE AND FOLLOW THE

B5286 TO HAWKSHEAD
WATERING HOLES: PLENTIFUL IN HAWKSHEAD

FAR TO NEAR SAWREY

Town End, Hill Top, Tower Bank Arms, Dub How Farm, Garnett Wood

12KM S OF AMBLESIDE. QUIET COUNTRYSIDE OF
WOODED HILL AND DALE, TWIXT ESTHWAITE WATER
AND WINDERMERE LAKE. THIS ROUND LEADS PAST
BEATRIX POTTER'S HILL TOP AND TOWER BANK ARMS,
UNCHANGED SINCE PETER RABBIT HIMSELF HOPPED
BY. A GENTLE STROLL SOAKS IN THE ATMOSPHERE
OF THIS DELIGHTFUL POCKET OF LAKELAND.

STEP BY STEP

▶ Beatrix Potter created a timeless image of Lakeland with her Peter Rabbit and animal character series of children's books The scenes she painted were based on the real landscape surrounding her home of Hill Top as well as other natural beauty spots of the Lake District. Walking by Hill Top, with the advantage of less crowded parking facilities, this walk makes a quiet exploration of a region that provided much of her inspiration.

Hill Top, home of Beatrix Potter

▶ Walk down the hill, passing the Sawrey Hotel on the right, to bear left towards Town End and St Peter's Church. Before the houses on the right a kissing gate leads to a path across meadows. Follow the path, crossing a little stone slab bridge and continue to gain the fenced path beneath the road. Follow this to emerge onto the road and bear left, to pass Hill Top and the Tower bank Arms, continuing on through the delightful village of Near Sawrey.

▶ Take the surfaced road to the left and turn left again at the next junction, to keep along the road, with fine views over the end of

Junction of ways below Near Sawrey

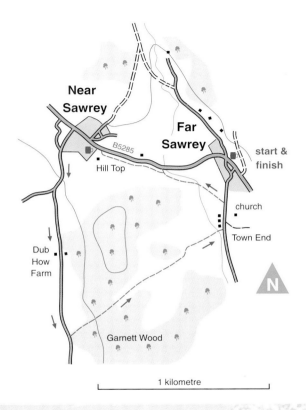

Near Sawrey

Far Sawrey

B5285

Hill Top

start & finish

church

Town End

Dub How Farm

Garnett Wood

N

1 kilometre

Crossing meadows to Near Sawrey

Garnett Wood

Esthwaite Water to the distant fells. At the next junction, beneath mighty oak and ash, go left to pass Dub How Farm, until a double stile (signed) on the left leads into the woods.

▶ A narrow, rough and often boggy path, leads up through the delightful Garnett Wood. At the top of the wood a stile leads into the fields and the path continues on to become a track. Take the high grassy track beneath the copse before descending to a little footbridge. The road by Town End is gained in a little way.

WALK 50 FACT FILE

LENGTH: 4.5KM
TIME: 1½ HOURS
DIFFICULTY: EASY; WITH A SHORT SECTION OF STRENUOUS ASCENT
START & FINISH: FAR SAWREY

VILLAGE HALL CAR PARK (379 954)
MAPS: OS L96 OR OL7
ACCESS: FROM AMBLESIDE FOLLOW THE A593 CONISTON ROAD TO TURN LEFT AT CLAPPERSGATE AND FOLLOW THE B5286.

TURN LEFT AT HAWKSHEAD TO FIND FAR SAWREY IN A FURTHER 4KM
WATERING HOLES: SAWREY HOTEL OPPOSITE START AND TOWER BANK ARMS IN NEAR SAWREY

TO THE HEAD OF KENTMERE

Hartrigg Farm, Reservoir Cottage, Kentmere Reservoir, Tongue House, Overend, Low Lane, Rook Howe

INTRODUCTION

7KM N OF STAVELEY. THE HEAD OF THE LONG KENTMERE VALLEY, BETWEEN CRAG QUARTER AND HOLLOW BANK QUARTER, COMPLETE WITH ITS RESERVOIR AND IMPRESSIVE MOUNTAIN SCENERY, PRESENTS STARK CONTRAST WITH THE GREENER LANDS BELOW. THIS ROUTE MAKES A CLOCKWISE CIRCUIT OF THE UPPER VALLEY, ASCENDING THE WEST SIDE AND RETURNING BY THE EAST

STEP BY STEP

▶ Follow the lane which leads off the road from the left side of the church. Head north along this to bear left over a boulder-strewn hill to join the surfaced road by the cattle grid. Go right along the road until, with Hartrigg farm down to the right, it becomes unsurfaced. Take the gate and continue along the track, passing a fine stand of Scots Pine to the right. Keep along the stony track, continuing beneath the steeps of Rainsbarrow Crag to the banks of slate by Reservoir Cottage. Slate waste and gaping quarry holes sunk deep into the flanks of Yoke bear testimony to a once important industry. Locally the slate hereabouts is known as "Pheasant Eye" – inspection will reveal the eyes.

▶ Continue along the track to the dam which forms Kentmere Reservoir. Two foot-bridges cross right, first across

A view to Rainsbarrow Crag

the dam overflow slipway and then over the River Kent. After crossing turn right and follow the track above the east bank of the river.

Over Overend to the head of Kentmere

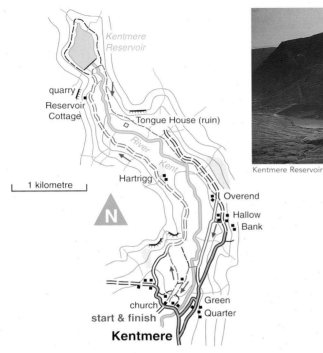

Kentmere Reservoir

quarry
Reservoir Cottage

Tongue House (ruin)

River Kent

1 kilometre

Hartrigg

Overend

Hallow Bank

N

church
start & finish
Kentmere

Green Quarter

Kentmere Reservoir

North to Tongue Scar

▶ Beyond the quarry spoil the track bears off left to pass beneath the little crag of Tongue Scar and by an ancient settlement marked by a few boulders and earthworks, before reaching the stone barn and ruin of Tongue House. Pass by the ruin and keep along the track to the buildings of Overend. Keep low and right, following the track to cross a little footbridge, to join the narrow walled way of Low Lane.

▶ Crest the hill to find a stone stile over the wall to the right. Cross this, passing a split boulder, to make descent to a footbridge. Beyond the bridge a squeeze stile leads out onto a lane. Go left and continue on past the buildings of Rook Howe farm, keeping along the left track to emerge onto the surfaced road just beneath Kentmere Church.

WALK 51 FACT FILE

LENGTH: 10km
TIME: 3½ hours
DIFFICULTY: Moderate; straightforward and mainly level going
START & FINISH: Limited parking by Kentmere Church (456 041)

MAPS: OS L90 or OL7
ACCESS: Staveley lies some 6km N of Kendal off the A591. Head N from Staveley along the narrow road which leads to Kentmere Church (To avoid parking problems a bus service – The Kentmere Rambler – makes regular runs from Staveley (Kendal and Ambleside) to Kentmere Church on summer Sundays and bank holidays – tel 01946 63222)

WATERING HOLES: Nearest are in Staveley – Wilf's Cafe, The Duke William, Eagle and Child Inn

STAVELY TO POTTER TARN ABOVE KENTDALE
(WITH POSSIBLE EXTENSION TO GURNAL DUBS)

Craggy Plantation, Littlewood Farm, Birk Field, Potter Tarn, (Gurnal Dubs), Hundhowe, Hagg Foot, River Kent

STAVELEY. THE EASTERN FELLS OF THE LAKE DISTRICT FALL TO KENTDALE NEAR THE ONCE INDUSTRIOUS LITTLE TOWN OF STAVELEY. ASCENDING BY CRAGGY PLANTATION THIS EXCELLENT AND VARIED WALK CLIMBS TO POTTER TARN, WITH POSSIBLE EXTENSION TO GURNAL DUBS, BEFORE FALLING TO CROSS AND TRAVERSE THE BANK OF THE RIVER KENT BACK TO STAVELEY.

STEP BY STEP

▶ Contrasting sylvan splendour by the River Kent, with high open fell side this is a revealing and varied walk. Return to the main street through Staveley and turn left (south) to find a narrow lane leading off left between the Duke William pub and the ancient St Margaret's Church Tower.

▶ Take the footbridge across the Kent and bear right by the river until a path splits off left towards the farm buildings. Pass these to find, beyond the barn on the left, a kissing gate and path leading up a little wooded field. Continue to a surfaced road and bear right, then left at the junction, to climb the hill until, at a bend in the road a kissing gate leads off left into Craggy Plantation. Bear right following the path through the woods of beech and oak until it finally rises, to make zigzag ascent.

▶ At the top of the wood bear left, until a short descent leads via a stile to open hillside. Take the gap in the wall and follow up the centre of the field. Cross the hill via a series of ladder stiles and continue down to Littlewood Farm.

▶ Bear right and follow the road until an open lane leads left down the hill to the cottage and buildings of Birk Field. Take the gate and pass

St Margaret's Church Tower

Looking up the River Kent from the bridge below Hagg Foot

in front of the cottage following the path out right by the little stream to rise and intercept a track. Bear right for a few metres then ascend the path left up the open hillside littered with boulders. Go right through the gap in the wall and then left through the gate and follow the path (with a spectacular view back to the Lakeland Fells behind) to pass Potter Tarn (reservoir) and then the end of the dam. (An extension to the walk leads on

below the dam, crossing over a stile to gain a path which rises up the open fell, cross a ladder stile at the top of the hill, and then down to the Gurnal Dubs.) Follow a grassy track down to the right of the stream which issues from the dam and continue down this to pass above Ghyll Pool and on to a junction of ways. Bear right, following the narrow lane to pass the buildings of Hundhowe and down to the road. Go right to pass Hagg Foot then left to gain a track. This leads to a bridge which crosses the River Kent. Follow the path along the west bank, beautiful woods, continuing until, at a bend in the river, the way leads off left (signed) to follow a path before intercepting a lane. Go right to gain the road and right again to Staveley.

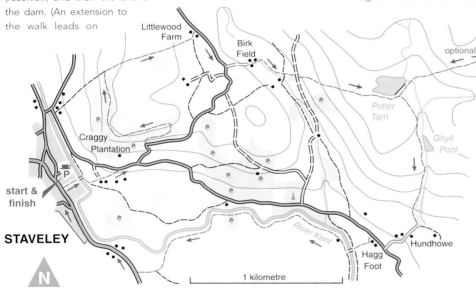

Littlewood Farm

Birk Field

optional

Gurnal Dubs

Potter Tarn

Ghyll Pool

Craggy Plantation

start & finish

STAVELEY

River Kent

Hundhowe

Hagg Foot

1 kilometre

N

Gurnal Dubs Reservoir

WALK 52 FACT FILE

LENGTH: 9KM (10.5KM WITH EXT)
TIME: 3½ HOURS (4 HOURS WITH EXT)
DIFFICULTY: DIFFICULT; WITH STEEPISH SECTIONS OF ASCENT AND DESCENT
START & FINISH: STAVELEY, THE OLD WOOD YARD OPPOSITE WILF'S CAFE (471 983)
MAPS: OS L97 OR OL7
ACCESS: STAVELEY LIES SOME 6KM N OF KENDAL OFF THE A591

WATERING HOLES: WILF'S CAFE, THE DUKE WILLIAM, EAGLE AND CHILD INN EN ROUTE

OVER WHITBARROW SCAR RISING BY CHAPEL HEAD

Chapel Head Scar, Lord's Seat, Farrer's Allotment, Mill Scar, Buckhouse Wood, Beck Head

INTRODUCTION

18KM SW OF KENDAL. S OF THE LAKELAND FELLS THE LONG, HIGH LIMESTONE ESCARPMENT OF WHITBARROW SCAR POINTS DIRECTLY TO MILNTHORPE SANDS. EXPLORING AN AREA OF OUTSTANDING FLORA AND FAUNA THIS ROUTE RISES BY THE CLIFFS OF CHAPEL HEAD SCAR AND FALLS TO BECK HEAD BY THOSE OF MILL SCAR.

STEP BY STEP

▶ An outstanding walk of exceptional interest; contrasting secret sylvan dale, the crystal-clear waters of the resurgence at Beck Head, skeletal white limestone with wonderful open vistas. Beyond the buildings, at the end of the track, enter and cross the field. Follow the footpath to pass a football field and continue to take the stile into Chapel Head Wood. Go left along the track and bear to the right until, under a yew tree, a path climbs steeply up the hillside. Beyond the trees continue on, to make open diagonal ascent. Cross a wooden stile over the higher stone wall. Traverse left above the wall rising to a cairned point. Go right to the obvious high point and little edge of limestone and walled stones which form a bench, Lord's Seat, the summit of Whitbarrow Scar. A beehive cairn stands just to the NW.

▶ Head S along the crest of the escarpment, following a natural highway. Take a stile through the wall, cross a dip and pass a gate to keep along the edge. Pass the edge of Farrer's Allotment on the left and continue to the end of the fence line, then bear left.

▶ At the junction of the ways, with the Kent Estuary dead ahead, bear right, taking the obvious path down through the silver birch and hazel

North over Whitbarrow Scar to the Langdale Pikes

Beneath Chapel Head Scar

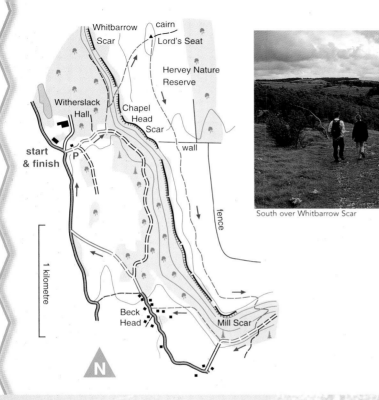

South over Whitbarrow Scar

(beware of the Destroying Angel mushroom – deadly poisonous) to find a gap in the stone wall. Pass through the gap, then go left. Pass through another gap in the wall, and continue to make diagonal descent down the limestone hillside. Intercept a horizontal track and bear right. Pass a natural spring then turn left (waymarked) on a constructed path descending steeply to a main track.

▶ Go right and keep right along the track until a path leads left, by the wall, across the field to pass through a gate and to the houses of Beck Head, to join a surfaced road. Below to the left is the remarkable resurgence of Beck Head and a short detour left along the road, to see it, is well rewarded. Go right along the road to pass through a gate, at which point the road becomes an unsurfaced track. Keep straight along the bridleway (passing the junctions) to join a surfaced road. Bear right along this.

Beck Head

WALK 53 FACT FILE

LENGTH: 7km
TIME: 3½ hours
DIFFICULTY: Difficult; with steep ascent and descent above unprotected cliffs
START & FINISH: Parking opposite

the old dog kennels of Witherslack Hall (437 860)
MAPS: OS L97 or OL7
ACCESS: Head S from Kendal along the A591, then W along the A590 to turn off right to Witherslack. Turn

right along a minor road to Town End and continue to a point just before Witherslack Hall Farm
WATERING HOLES: None en route, Derby Arms Inn off A590 nearby

BY FINSTHWAITE'S HIGH DAM AND RUSLAND WOODS

High Dam, Rusland Heights, Crosslands, Rusland Cross, Rusland Beeches, July Flowertree, Finsthwaite

18KM SW OF WINDERMERE. LYING WEST OF THE BOTTOM OF WINDERMERE LAKE, BETWEEN LITTLE FINSTHWAITE AND THE RUSLAND VALLEY, THE TREE CLAD RUSLAND HEIGHTS REMAIN A QUIET LAKELAND BACKWATER. THIS ANTICLOCKWISE ROUND PASSES HIGH DAM TO SCALE THE HEIGHTS BEFORE RETURNING AROUND THE BASE OF THEIR SOUTHERN PERIMETER.

STEP BY STEP

The road section along the Rusland Valley is greatly enhanced by the awesome presence of the long line of ancient Rusland Beeches which thankfully, due to an upsurge of public opinion, survived a campaign to have them felled in the late 1990's. Ascend the track above the car park continuing to pass the pond of Low Dam (which lies to the left). Gain the dam wall and turn left along it, to follow a footpath above the edge of the waters of High Dam. Take the path ascending left through the trees. Keep left and continue in ascent until it moves out onto the open top of Rusland Heights.

Keep along the grassy path, with lovely stands of silver birch, until with magnificent views out to the Lakeland Fells, a notched boulder by the path marks a steepening descent into the Rusland valley. Follow the path, occasional waymarks and marker posts, to gain the surfaced road. Go left and keep left at Crosslands to pass through the

The famed Rusland beeches

View to the fells from notched boulder on Rusland Heights

buildings of Rusland Cross (keep straight on at the junction).

▶ Continue along the road until woods manifest to the left and the long line of beeches begin. Their great silver trunks, both smooth and knotted, stand like huge imperial elephants – long may they reign. Go left at the junction ascending until a gate leads to a track on the left. Follow the track to a gate and veer left along by the stone wall. Cross Black Beck and follow the ancient track over a rise to make descent to the Finsthwaite road. Go left along the road, passing the buildings of Town End and on past Tom Heights and July Flowertree descending into the hamlet of Finsthwaite. Keep left to find the track climbing back up to the car park.

High Dam dam

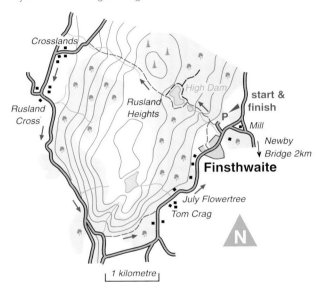

High Dam Reservoir, Rusland Heights

WALK 54 FACT FILE

LENGTH: 10KM
TIME: 3½ HOURS
DIFFICULTY: DIFFICULT; WITH MODERATELY STRENUOUS ASCENT AND DESCENT
START & FINISH: FINSTHWAITE'S HIGH DAM CAR PARK (368 882)
MAPS: OS L97 OR OL7
ACCESS: FOLLOW THE A592 S FROM WINDERMERE. TURN RIGHT ONTO THE A590 AT NEWBY BRIDGE AND RIGHT AGAIN, TAKING THE BRIDGE OVER THE RIVER LEVEN. PASS THE SWAN HOTEL AND TURN LEFT. GO RIGHT AT THE NEXT JUNCTION AND CONTINUE THROUGH FINSTHWAITE
WATERING HOLES: NONE EN ROUTE, THE SWAN HOTEL AT NEWBY BRIDGE NEARBY

A CIRCUIT AROUND BRANTWOOD ABOVE CONISTON WATER

Brantwood, Pen Intake, Lawson Park, Shepherd's Cottage, Cock Point

5KM S OF CONISTON. THE WOODED FLANKS OF CRAG HEAD AND THE ENVIRONS OF LAWSON PARK FARM, WHICH OVERLOOKS RUSKIN'S BRANTWOOD AND CONISTON WATER, THOUGH ENCROACHED UPON BY AFFORESTATION, STILL OFFER SPECTACULAR VIEWS TO THE CONISTON OLD MAN MASSIF. A WALK BY CONISTON WATER AND THE HEIGHTS ABOVE BRANTWOOD.

STEP BY STEP

▶ Bear right along the road, peaceful views over wood and meadow to the lake and beyond, to pass the fine house and gardens of Brantwood, home of John Ruskin between 1872 and 1900. Continue along the road until it climbs to pass the drive to Low Bank Ground on the left, and gain a gate into the woods on the right (signposted 'Public Bridleway').

▶ Follow the track, rising through mixed woods to emerge into the open by Pen Intake. Keep low along the track to re-enter woods before climbing once again to ascend the flanks of Crag Head. At a crest in the hill a curious curving wooden barrel bench on the right provides some respite

Brantwood by Coniston Water

before the going levels. Pass an old stone barn and continue into the dip to rise again. Bear right at a point where a wide Forestry Track is intercepted, to the fine old buildings of Lawson Park Farm. Since the advent of Grizedale Forest this has been abandoned as a farm and consequently little has changed since. The position, high above Coniston Water, is quite magnificent and the views across to Dow Crag, Coniston Old Man and Wetherlam simply breathtaking.

The view over Coniston Water from Brantwood

Pass the farm to find, on the right, an old track dropping down through the forestry. The track descends directly at first then bears left to traverse through the woods of Machell Coppice, making slow descent to the road. En route, just right of the track, partially hidden and surrounded by a dense thicket of tree and bush, stands a deserted shepherd's cottage – a secret hideaway featured in Arthur Ransome's *Swallows and Amazons*.

Bear right along the road, passing Cock Point, with wonderful proximity to the silvery reflections of Coniston Water.

Hideaway cottage in Machell Coppice

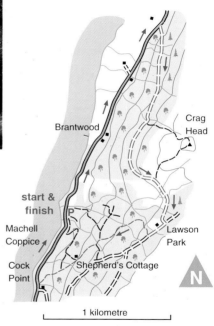

Mixed woods below Crag Head

Lawson Park Farm

WALK 55 FACT FILE

LENGTH: 6KM
TIME: 2 HOURS
DIFFICULTY: MODERATE; STRAIGHTFORWARD ASCENT AND DESCENT ON ROUGH TRACKS

START & FINISH: MACHELL COPPICE CAR PARK BY BECK LEVEN FOOT (310 952)
MAPS: OS L96 OR OL7
ACCESS: TAKE THE MINOR ROAD BEARING RIGHT OFF THE B5285 FROM THE HEAD OF

CONISTON WATER TO RUN DOWN THE EAST SIDE (BACK) OF THE LAKE
WATERING HOLES: NONE EN ROUTE, PLENTIFUL IN CONISTON

TO LEVERS WATER AND THE COPPERMINES VALLEY

Walna Scar Road, The Pudding Stone, Boulder Valley, Levers Water, Coppermines Valley, Miners Bridge

INTRODUCTION

CONISTON. HIGH AMIDST THE RUGGED MOUNTAIN GRANDEUR OF CONISTON OLD MAN THE EXTENSIVE WORKINGS WITHIN THE COPPERMINES VALLEY NOW LIE MAINLY SILENT. TAKING A HIGH-LEVEL ROUTE FROM THE ANCIENT WALNA SCAR ROAD VIA THE BOULDER VALLEY, TO ENCIRCLE LEVERS WATER, THIS ROUTE DESCENDS THE COPPERMINES VALLEY BEFORE CROSSING MINERS BRIDGE AND MAKING RE-ASCENT.

STEP BY STEP

▶ In addition to the many employed in slate quarrying, the characterful village of Coniston was once home for some six hundred men who worked the copper mines.

High in the stark confines of the Coppermines Valley, overshadowed by mountain finery unbowed, their spoilings remain. Take the quarry track running off the Walna Scar Road northwards above the gate. Beyond the rocky hillock of The Bell (whose short scrambly ascent provides a commanding view over the Coppermines Valley) the track makes a hairpin turn to the left to begin its ascent of Coniston Old Man.

Quarry track leading by The Bell

▶ After 100m take another stony quarry track traversing off to the right. At its end follow the path traversing the hillside to pass the great boulder of The Pudding Stone before falling slightly to cross Low Water beck. The path continues to make gentle ascent up the natural rift of Boulder Valley to overlook the dark dammed waters of Levers Water. Keep away from the edge of the gaping mineshaft (near the top of Simon's Nick) and do not venture into any tunnels – they are all potentially dangerous

Levers Water nestling below Coniston Old Man

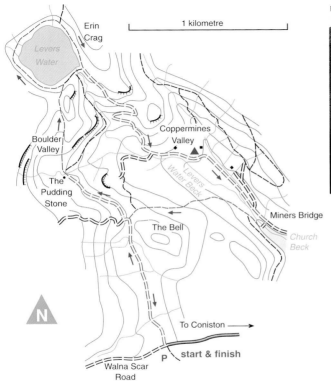

Reflections on Levers Water

A view up the beck into Coppermines Valley

however innocent they may appear.

► Bear left and follow the rough path which circumnavigates the tarn. Beyond the dam spillway, a track leads down into the depths of the Coppermines Valley. Follow the track and go along the banks of spoil to pass the Youth Hostel.

► Continue to follow the unsurfaced stony road leading out of the valley. The track runs along to intercept Church Beck just above the waterfalls. Though a wet crossing can be made to gain a stile on the opposite bank it is probably best to descend the little way to the masonry Miners Bridge which spans the gorge. Go right across the bridge and right again to follow the path which ascends to join the original quarry track at the hairpin bend by The Bell.

WALK 56 FACT FILE

LENGTH: 8KM

TIME: 2½ HOURS

DIFFICULTY: MODERATE; SOME ROUGH GOING (DANGEROUS MINESHAFTS)

START & FINISH: PARKING ABOVE THE GATE OFF THE WALNA SCAR ROAD (289 970)

MAPS: OS L96 OR OL6

ACCESS: TAKE THE ROAD RISING STEEPLY, ABOVE THE PETROL STATION, FROM CONISTON TO GAIN THE UNSURFACED WALNA SCAR ROAD (USED BY QUARRY TRAFFIC)

WATERING HOLES: NONE EN ROUTE, PLENTIFUL IN CONISTON

TO BEACON TARN AND THE BEACON ATOP BLAWITH FELL

Fairholme Green, Slatestone Fell, Beacon Knott, The Beacon, Blawith Wood Bottom

8.5 KM S OF CONISTON. THE ROUGH BRACKENED SLOPES OF BLAWITH FELL STAND WEST OF THE FOOT OF CONISTON LAKE AND RISE TO A COMMANDING VIEWPOINT – THE BEACON. THIS ROUTE MAKES A CLOCKWISE CIRCUIT TO APPROACH THE TOP OF THE FELL VIA BEACON TARN BEFORE DESCENDING IN A NORTHERLY DIRECTION TOWARDS STABLE HARVEY.

STEP BY STEP

▶ A narrow though well defined path rises up the brackened hillside on the opposite side of the road to the SW of the lay-by pull off. Cross the road and pass a group of juniper bushes and a little stream. Beyond a little grove of bushes bear left to climb the path steeply up the hillside. Approaching overhead power lines the way moves left to circumnavigate the flanks of Slatestone Fell, then falls to join a wider path/track in a little valley.

By the footbridge beyond Slatestone Fell

▶ Go right to cross the footbridge and make ascent, over a rock slab outcrop. Beyond this a path cuts right over the outlet stream directly to the banks of Beacon Tarn – a lovely quiet stretch of water with white water lilies to its northern end. Ascend the shoulder to its right, Bleak Knott, which is boggy in places, to gain the rocky knoll summit of Blawith Fell – The Beacon. It isn't difficult to understand why this point was chosen to site a beacon. The view is quite astonishing. Stretching from

Autumn colours Beacon Tarn

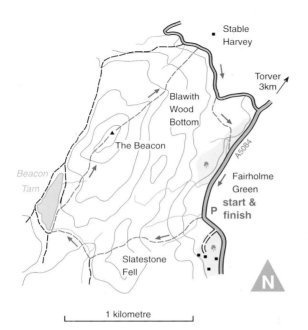

Stable Harvey

Torver 3km

Blawith Wood Bottom

The Beacon

Beacon Tarn

A5084

Fairholme Green

start & finish

P

Slatestone Fell

N

1 kilometre

View to Coniston Water from The Beacon

Ascending the rock slab

Tranquil Beacon Tarn

Morecambe Bay it includes the entire length of Coniston Lake to the distant central and eastern fells, and offers particulary fine aspect to Dow Crag and Coniston Old Man.

Take the path running down the shoulder of Blawith Wood Bottom and continue to the surfaced road which leads to Stable Harvey Farm. Bear right down the road until at a bend, a footpath bears off right (signed) to pass through Brown Howe Woods and join the A5084.

WALK 57 FACT FILE

LENGTH: 5KM
TIME: 2 HOURS
DIFFICULTY: MODERATE; BOGGY IN PLACES WITH SHORT STEEPISH SECTIONS OF ASCENT

START & FINISH: LAY-BY AT BLAWITH COMMON (287 903)
MAPS: OS L96 OR OL6
ACCESS: FOLLOW THE A593 S FROM CONISTON TO TORVER. TURN LEFT ALONG

THE A5084 AND FOLLOW THE W SIDE OF CONISTON WATER TO THE OPEN GROUND OF BLAWITH COMMON
WATERING HOLES: NONE EN ROUTE, FARMERS ARMS AT LOWICK NEARBY

OVER BLAWITH KNOTT AND TOTTLEBANK HEIGHT

Giant's Grave, Blawith Knott, Tottlebank Tarn, Tottlebank Height, Round Haw, High Kep, Mere Sike, Lang Tarn

10KM NE OF BROUGHTON IN FURNESS. WITH COMMANDING POSITION OVER THE DUDDON ESTUARY, THESE LITTLE FELLS N OF KIRKBY MOOR, DISPLAY MANY RELICS OF PREHISTORY. THIS ANTICLOCKWISE ROUTE TRAVERSES THE HEIGHTS BEYOND BLAWITH KNOTT.

STEP BY STEP

There can't be too many pull offs that include a prehistoric burial mound as an added extra. But this one does; a circular embankment marks the first evidence of prehistory which abounds on these quiet fells. Pass the mound and descend the road to

Ancient earthwork, Blawith Knott beyond

pass the track, public bridleway to Tottlebank, and on over the stream. Leaving the road a grassy path climbs to the right to pass the rather indistinct, though grandly named, stones and hollow of Giant's Grave, lying just to the left. A narrow though well-defined path leads all the way up the shoulder to the small cairn marking the summit of Blawith Knott.

The path continues to lead down the shoulder and then bears right over level ground to the tiny Tottlebank Tarn. Bear right to ascend Tottlebank Height for a view to Coniston Water. Head north steeply down the shoulder and continue to descend Round Haw bearing left to cross a little stream and down to the bottom of the little valley to join the ancient bridleway, from Cockenskell to Woodland, at a point where it crosses another little stream. Turn left and ascend to the col of High Kep, at which point the stream of Mere Sike enters from the left.

Looking from the heights beyond Blawith Knott

Atop Tottlebank Height

Sunset over Duddon Sands

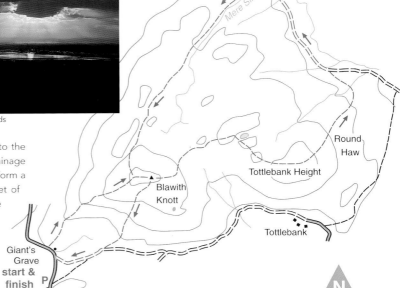

▶ Bear left and climb the heather-clad hillside following a path to the right of the stream. Continue along to the right of the stream/drainage channel. A ridge of higher ground rises immediately to the right to form a natural corridor over the moss. Keep along this to pass the droplet of Lang Tarn, and out though a ravine in the flanks of the hill to the shoulder of Blawith Knott.

▶ The open vista of Duddon Sands appears suddenly in front. A path leads directly down the steep hillside, following the line marked on the map of the Parish Boundary, to gain the edge of a flat bog. The bridleway to Tottlebank lies at the far side though it is best to go right and circumnavigate the bog to gain the high dry shoulder just above the road by Giant's Grave.

Map labels: High Kep, Mere Sike, Round Haw, Tottlebank Height, Blawith Knott, Tottlebank, Giant's Grave **start & finish** P, 1 kilometre, N

WALK 58 FACT FILE

LENGTH: 6KM
TIME: 2½ HOURS
DIFFICULTY: MODERATE; BOGGY AND ROUGH GOING IN PLACES WITH SHORT THOUGH STEEPISH SECTIONS OF ASCENT
START & FINISH: PULL OFF ON LONG RIGG HILL (256 878)
MAPS: OS L96 OR OL6
ACCESS: FROM BROUGHTON GO E TO JOIN THE A595 TO GRIZEBECK THEN FOLLOW THE A5092 RISING TO THE TOP OF KIRKBY MOOR. A MINOR ROAD LEADS N FROM THE HEIGHTS OF THE MOOR AND IS FOLLOWED TO PASS OVER THE SUMMIT OF LONG RIGG HILL
WATERING HOLES: NONE EN ROUTE, PLENTIFUL IN BROUGHTON NEARBY, GALLERY CAFE AT SKELWITH BRIDGE

ROUNDING THE EAST DUNNERDALE FELLS FROM KILN BANK CROSS

Park Head Road (bridleway), Long Mire, Jackson Ground, Whinscars, The Knott, Slate Quarries

INTRODUCTION

6KM N OF BROUGHTON IN FURNESS. THE LITTLE DUNNERDALE VALLEY CUTS THROUGH THE WILD AND RUGGED FELLS WHICH RUN BETWEEN THE DUDDON VALLEY AND THE VALE OF LICKLE. THIS EXPLORATION OF ITS EASTERN FELLS, WITH A VISIT OUT TO THE VIEWPOINT OF THE KNOTT, MAKES A CLOCKWISE CIRCUIT AROUND THE HEIGHTS OF FOX HAW AND RAVEN'S CRAG.

STEP BY STEP

▶ Despite labelling to the contrary on OS maps, Dunnerdale is a separate little valley. It runs through remote and fascinating terrain to form a pass between Hall Dunnerdale and Broughton Mills. Take the high path which runs left (N) from the parking area, and descends to join the grassy track and ancient bridleway known as the Park Head Road. Go left and follow it until, with a stone wall and the rocky knoll of Brock Barrow to the left, a rise offers a surprise view over the Duddon Valley to the high fells.

▶ Make descent to cross the stream, Old Park Beck, then take the grassy path/ track ascending to the right. Continue over the col to pass through the corridor of Long Mire, many piles of boulders indicate relics of prehistory, to bear left in descent. At a pile of stones, which resemble an ancient burial chamber, and before crossing the little stream of Broadslack Beck, a path cuts off the track down to the right. Follow the path and cross the beck (easy) to recross it again below its confluence with Long Mire Beck. Continue to the corner of the stone wall and follow the grassy track above to the right. Keep along the track to pass Jackson Ground and continue, to round the rocky spur of Whinscars with the buildings of Carter

Over Duddon Valley to High Fells

Dunnerdale ascending to Kiln Bank Cross

Ground down below. As the track begins to ascend, almost hidden in the bracken, old mine workings can be seen (unfenced).

▶ Ascend to a bend in the track and then go left, across the foundations of the old wall, and out to The Knott. A revealing view out across The Duddon Estuary. Return to the track and bear left (N) keeping right along the higher track to traverse the flanks of the hillside above the valley of Dunnerdale. Follow the track until a path descends left, to skirt a stone wall, and cross a beck before rising up the bank of slate quarry spoil. The path cuts up the hillside to the right, crossing the quarried rift at a closure (care – unfenced), and rises back to Kiln Bank Cross.

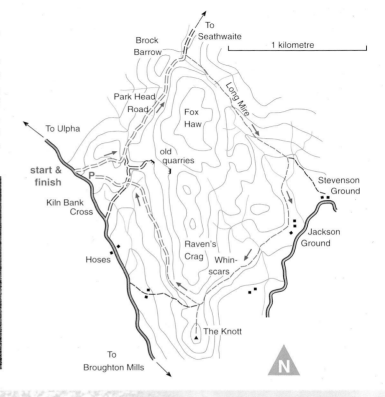

A slatey outcrop above Kiln Bank Cross

Herdwich sheep near The Knott

WALK 59 FACT FILE

LENGTH: 6.5KM
TIME: 2 HOURS
DIFFICULTY: MODERATE; FAIRLY LEVEL GOING ON REASONABLY GOOD TRACKS (PASSING UNFENCED QUARRY AND MINE HOLES)

START & FINISH: KILN BANK CROSS (215 933)
MAPS: OS L96 OR OL6
ACCESS: FOLLOW THE A593 N FROM BROUGHTON BEFORE TAKING THE MINOR ROAD LEFT TO BROUGHTON MILLS. GO LEFT

TO ASCEND THE VALLEY OF DUNNERDALE (GATE ABOVE HOSES) TO THE HEAD OF THE PASS – KILN BANK CROSS
WATERING HOLES: NONE EN ROUTE, THE BLACKSMITH'S ARMS IN BROUGHTON MILLS NEARBY

BY THE DUDDON'S WALLOWBARROW CRAG AND GORGE

Seathwaite Church, High Wallowbarrow Farm, Wallowbarrow Crag, Rowantree How, Grassguards,
Wallowbarrow Gorge

INTRODUCTION

**11KM N OF BROUGHTON IN FURNESS. WHERE THE
RIVER TUMBLES THROUGH WALLOWBARROW GORGE
TO GENTLER PASTURES BELOW, WHERE ROCKY CRAG
AND MIXED WOODS GIVE WAY TO GENTLER CLIMES;
HERE LIES THE ENCHANTING WORLD OF THE MIDDLE
DUDDON. FOLLOWING A CLOCKWISE COURSE THIS
ROUTE ASCENDS BY WALLOWBARROW CRAG AND
DESCENDS BY GRASSGUARDS TO MAKE RETURN
THROUGH WALLOWBARROW GORGE**

Autumn colours on the edge of Wallowbarrow Woods

STEP BY STEP

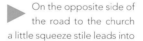 If there be elves they live here in these magical woods by the River Duddon. Huge piles of twigs and tree debris bear testimony to the fact that large wood ants certainly do. This, a walk for all seasons, presents a kaleidoscope of colour in autumn. If parking space isn't available an alternative start can be made from the Newfield Inn (parking for patrons), or even High Wallowbarrow Farm (by missing out the Seathwaite leg).

A view to Wallowbarrow Crag

On the opposite side of the road to the church a little squeeze stile leads into the field above Tarn Beck. Follow the footpath and go right over the wooden footbridge. The path bears left and the trees open before closing in again, beyond which the path descends to the stone arch of Wallowbarrow Bridge.

Take the bridge over the River Duddon, or more adventurously the stepping stones found a little further downstream. From the bridge continue through the woods, bearing slightly left, to gain a gate which exits the wood into an open field. Keep along to the red granite buildings of High Wallowbarrow Farm (noted for its exotic animals) and turn right to follow the track which rises by the side of Wallowbarrow Crag. Keep along

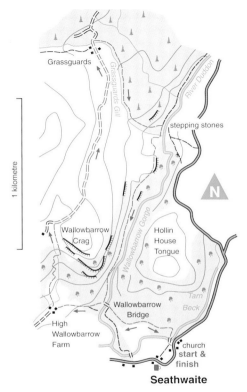

Grassguards

Grassguards Gill

River Duddon

stepping stones

1 kilometre

N

Wallowbarrow Crag

Wallowbarrow Gorge

Hollin House Tongue

Tarn Beck

Wallowbarrow Bridge

High Wallowbarrow Farm

church
start & finish

Seathwaite

Wallowbarrow Bridge

The oaks of Wallowbarrow Woods

By silver birch

this track over Rowantree How – noting the careful precision of the stone walling – to the buildings and houses of Grassguards.

 Cross the ford then leave the track to take the path which descends to the right above Grassguards Gill. A section of steep rocky descent leads to the River Duddon. Bear right and follow the path above the west bank of the river (above unfenced crags for a short way). Continue down through Wallowbarrow Gorge and back to Wallowbarrow Bridge.

WALK 60 FACT FILE

LENGTH: 6.5KM
TIME: 2½ HOURS
DIFFICULTY: MODERATE; SOME ROUGH GOING (UNFENCED STEEPS ABOVE THE GORGE) WITH STEEP THOUGH SHORT ASCENT AND DESCENT
START & FINISH: LIMITED PARKING OPPOSITE SEATHWAITE CHURCH (229 962)
MAPS: OS L96 OR OL6
ACCESS: FROM BROUGHTON FOLLOW THE A595 W TO DUDDON BRIDGE TO TURN RIGHT AND KEEP UP THE DUDDON ROAD THROUGH ULPHA AND SEATHWAITE
WATERING HOLES: NONE EN ROUTE, NEWFIELD INN AT SEATHWAITE NEARBY

BY SWINSIDE'S STONE CIRCLE AND WRAYSLACK

Beck Bank Farm Stepping Stones, Knott Moor, Swinside Circle, Fenwick, Thwaites Fell, Wrayslack, Graystone House

INTRODUCTION

3.5KM W OF BROUGHTON IN FURNESS. OCCUPYING A SECRETIVE VALLEY HIGH ABOVE THE DUDDON ESTUARY, SWINSIDE IS ONE OF THE MOST IMPRESSIVE STONE CIRCLES OF THE REGION. THIS WALK FOLLOWS A CLOCKWISE ROUTE RISING FROM BECK BANK FARM TO SWINDALE BEFORE TOUCHING ON THWAITES FELL AND DESCENDING VIA WRAYSLACK.

STEP BY STEP

▶ This intriguing round offers wonderful open vistas over The Duddon Estuary to the mountains of North Wales and Anglesey, and from the moorland of Thwaites Fell to the high Lakeland Fells. It passes Swinside Stone Circle and many other relics of prehistory en route. Follow by the side of the busy A595 west (wide verge) for 150m until a road leads off right to Broadgate. Continue, until a track on the right leads between the buildings of Beck Bank Farm to gain a path and stepping stones which cross little Black Beck.

Swinside Stone Circle

▶ Bear right then left, to ascend the field and gain the surfaced road. Turn right then left at the next junction, and follow the road which rises over the desolation of Knott Moor to Swinside Farm. The standing stones of Swinside Stone Circle, also known as Sunkenkirk, will be seen through a wooden gate to the right, just below the farm.

▶ Keep right to pass the farm and continue along a grassy track until a path bears down right to cross Peathouse Beck by a footbridge. Rise, to cross a stile on the right and continue across the fields via a vague path

South over Swinside Stone Circle and The Knott

54

to take the stiles over the stone walls (steps painted white at the time of writing). Join a track which leads directly to the farmyard at Fenwick. Bear right before the yard and buildings, and follow the track to gain a surfaced road. Turn right, above Windy Slack, and rise to intercept another road. Go left to a junction.

▶ At the meeting of ways bear right to leave the road and follow the grassy track and path across the open moorland of Thwaites Fell. Descend to intercept a grassy track above the stone wall. Keep left to pass by an old slate quarry. Rise to the brow of the hill then go right, through the gated gap in the wall to follow the vague track over the upper flanks of the hill of Wrayslack before making winding descent, with wonderful views over the estuary, to gain the surfaced road above Graystone House.

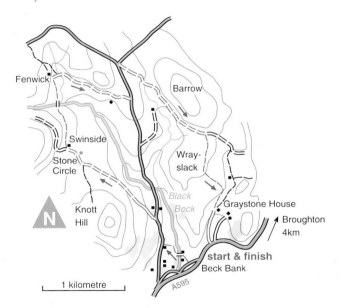

Stone stiles to Fenwick

Stepping stones over Black Beck

WALK 61 FACT FILE

LENGTH: 8.5KM
TIME: 3 HOURS
DIFFICULTY: DIFFICULT; MAINLY ON GOOD TRACKS AND PATHS WITH STEADY ASCENT AND DESCENT

START & FINISH: ABOVE THE JUNCTION OF THE GRAYSTONE HOUSE ROAD WITH THE A595 (187 870)
MAPS: OS L96 OR OL6
ACCESS: FOLLOW THE A595 W FROM

BROUGHTON, BEYOND THE LONG ASCENT FROM DUDDON BRIDGE FIND A WIDE JUNCTION WITH THE ROAD TO GRAYSTONE HOUSE
WATERING HOLES: NONE EN ROUTE, PLENTIFUL IN BROUGHTON

UPPER ESKDALE BY BROTHERILKELD

Brotherilkeld, Tongue Pot, Lingcove Bridge, Heron Stones, Scale Bridge, Taw House

20KM W OF AMBLESIDE. BENEATH THE SHADOW OF HARDKNOTT'S ROMAN FORT, UPPER ESKDALE BRANCHES OUT FROM THE CULTIVATED PASTURES BELOW TO ENTER INTO THE HEART OF A WILD MOUNTAIN KINGDOM. THIS ROUTE ASCENDS BY THE EAST SIDE OF THE VALLEY TO CROSS LINGCOVE BRIDGE BEFORE FORDING THE RIVER ESK TO RETURN BY THE OPPOSITE BANK.

STEP BY STEP

▶ The centrepiece of this beguiling walk into an imposing mountain world is undoubtably the young River Esk. Its crystal-clear waters, cascading waterfalls, tumbling rapids, deep green pools and polished rocks of light blue rhyolite, are the most blithe of any mountain beck imaginable.

▶ Follow the track to the farm of Brotherilkeld. Bear left to the riverbank just before the buildings are reached. In Old Norse (Viking), Keld means 'place by the river'. Two cultures seem to overlap here as this place was certainly farmed by the monks (brothers) of Furness. Who was 'Il'?

▶ Continue by the bank of the river. Note the cavernously exposed roots of the great oaks which bear witness to the frequency of high flooding, before the path bears away right to cross the fields. A grassy track passes through numerous piles of stones and earthworks before rising to a ladder stile (and gap) in the stone

Up the River Esk to Bowfell

Over Brotherilkeld to Upper Eskdale

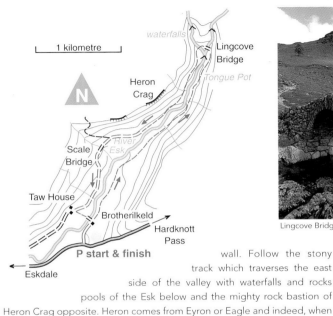

1 kilometre

N

waterfalls

Lingcove Bridge

Tongue Pot

Heron Crag

River Esk

Scale Bridge

Taw House

Brotherilkeld

Hardknott Pass

P start & finish

Eskdale

Lingcove Bridge

The red granite of Brotherilkeld Farm

wall. Follow the stony track which traverses the east side of the valley with waterfalls and rocks pools of the Esk below and the mighty rock bastion of Heron Crag opposite. Heron comes from Eyron or Eagle and indeed, when I was a child, the Golden Eagle used to nest here. The path intercepts the river by the long deep green pool of Tongue Pot – a perfect bathing pool, before continuing to the sheepfold and stone arched packhorse bridge of Lingcove Bridge.

▶ Bear left to make a crossing of the River Esk. If the water is high a crossing may not be feasible and return by the same route is the best option. Otherwise continue down the west bank of the river. Follow a grassy path to pass beneath Heron Crag and by the split rock of Heron Stones. The path rises rightwards by the wall to become a track. Cross Scale Bridge below the waterfall and continue to follow the track as it descends left through the fields and on to Taw House Farm. Enter the farm-yard then take the ladder stile to the left. Follow the path to cross the footbridge over the River Esk back to Brotherilkeld Farm.

WALK 62 FACT FILE

LENGTH: 6.5KM
TIME: 2¼ HOURS
DIFFICULTY: MODERATE; MAINLY ON GOOD PATHS/TRACKS THOUGH IT INCLUDES A RIVER CROSSING OVER THE RIVER ESK

START & FINISH: THE FOOT OF HARDKNOTT PASS, BY THE TELEPHONE BOX AT BROTHERILKELD (212 012) OR CAR PARKS A FEW HUNDRED METRES DOWN THE ROAD
MAPS: OS L89 OR OL6

ACCESS: FROM AMBLESIDE CROSS OVER WRYNOSE PASS AND HARDKNOTT PASS (SUMMER CONDITIONS ONLY) TO ESKDALE
WATERING HOLES: NONE EN ROUTE, WOOLPACK INN NEARBY

BY VALLEY AND FELL TO ESKDALE'S BLEA TARN

Church Stepping Stones, Boot, Bleatarn Hill, Blea Tarn, Siney Tarn, Fisherground Farm,
Milkingstead Bridge, Dalegarth Hall

INTRODUCTION

25KM W OF AMBLESIDE. TO THE NORTH OF MIDDLE
ESKDALE, COMPLETE WITH SECRETIVE TARNS AND
RELICS DATING FROM PREHISTORY, A FELL OF PINK
RED GRANITE OVERLOOKS THE SYLVAN TRACTS OF
THE VALLEY. TWICE CROSSING THE RIVER ESK, THIS
ROUTE RISES FROM THE VALLEY TO TRAVERSE THE
NORTHERN HEIGHTS IN A CLOCKWISE CIRCUIT.

INTRODUCTION

STEP BY STEP

▶ This delightfully varied round is overpowering in its visual splendour. Evidence of prehistory and of Roman occupation abound. Take the track which bears to the left of Dalegarth Hall. At the crossing of ways go left to cross the field. Take the footbridge over Stanley Gill. Follow the track until a footpath cuts down left. Cross the river by the stepping stones opposite the church. Take the track leading left away from the river. (Alternatively a footpath can be followed up the south bank of the river to gain a footbridge.) Follow the track to the main road, cross and take the road to Boot. Beyond the arched bridge, pass through the gate and follow the track which ascends to the right. With its cobbled pavement exposed in places this road climbs directly to the old 'Peat Houses' on the edge of Burnmoor.

▶ Take the left grassy track which leads up through the buildings and continue, to pass the exposed shaft which marks the top of the old haematite (iron) mines above Boot. Keep along this track, crossing the remains of a wall of once considerable size, to ascend the flanks of Bleatarn Hill. Although the main path keeps to the left of the

Stone wall to Boot

Over Blea Tarn to Blea Tarn Hill

summit to follow a sunken corridor, the flat top of the hill provides splendid views. Descend to the waters of Blea Tarn, fringed by rocky outcrops, and keep along the grassy track/path to swing right across its base. Relics of prehistory in the form of gathered stones lie to the SW.

▶ Continue along the grassy path, with tiny Blind Tarn over to the left, to skirt the side of boggy Siney Tarn. Circumnavigate Sineytarn Moss before the path splits. Go left. The grassy path/track is narrow and boggy in places, though with care can be followed to intercept a stone wall on the Eskdale side of the fell. The path leads above the wall, ignore the ladder stile, and along to a kissing gate. Keep high to the right (ancient holes above) to pick up a well-engineered track.

▶ Descend the track, pass through a gap in the wall, to take the path off down left by the fence. Stile into the wood.

Continue, to cross the Ravenglass and Eskdale Railway track – 'La'al Ratty' – and on past Fisherground to the main road. Take the path opposite and cross the River Esk by Milkingstead Bridge. Go left along the track and keep on through woods to pass Dalegarth Hall back to the crossing of ways and your starting point.

Eskdale Church

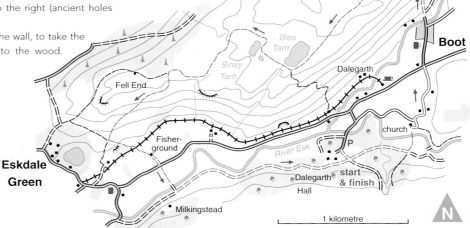

WALK 63 FACT FILE

LENGTH: 9.5KM
TIME: 3½ HOURS
DIFFICULTY: DIFFICULT; BOGGY IN PLACES ON HIGH GROUND
START & FINISH: CAR PARK NEAR DALEGARTH HALL (171 003)
MAPS: OS L96 & L89 OR OL6
ACCESS: FROM AMBLESIDE CROSS OVER WRYNOSE PASS AND HARDKNOTT PASS (SUMMER CONDITIONS ONLY) TO ESKDALE. TURN LEFT PAST DALEGARTH STATION
WATERING HOLES: BROOK HOUSE INN AND THE BURNMOOR INN AT BOOT EN ROUTE, DALEGARTH STATION NEARBY

OVER MUNCASTER FELL

Fell Lane, Hooker Crag, Ross's Camp, Muncaster Head, Roman Kilns, High Eskholme, Henry's Tower

18KM S OF EGREMONT. THE SHOULDER OF MUNCASTER FELL, A NATURAL STRATEGIC HIGHWAY AND ROMAN ROAD, RISES BETWEEN RAVENGLASS AND ESKDALE GREEN. ASCENDING FROM THE W TO TRAVERSE THE HEIGHTS, THIS ROUND MAKES A CLOCKWISE CIRCUIT TO RETURN BY A TRACK WHICH RUNS THROUGH LOWER ESKDALE BY THE FOOT OF THE FELL.

STEP BY STEP

▶ Following the line of the old Roman road which once led from the ancient port of Ravenglass to Eskdale this fascinating and rewarding walk offers wonderful views and position. Go left along the road. At the bend, continue straight up Fell Lane. Continue, to pass Muncaster Tarn hidden amongst the firs and rhododendrons to the left, until, past the end of the plantation, the craggy knoll of Hooker Crag rises to the left. Although the main track/path continues below to the right, it is worth the climb to top the summit of Muncaster Fell. Views extend to Scafell and out to the Isle of Man and Ireland beyond.

▶ Return to the track and continue to find a considerable granite slab balanced on stone uprights. Ross's Camp 1883 is chiselled neatly in the slab, though it is my opinion that these are the remains of a neolithic burial chamber – note that (hidden in the bracken) the whole structure is completely surrounded by a circle of standing stones some 22 metres in diameter. Continue along the track, to pass through a gap in the wall and descend, note the occasional granite standing stones flanking the track, into a dip below Silver Knott.

▶ The track first ascends to a rock cutting before making descent. Traversing down a structured embankment of granite masonry blocks, the ancient highway clings to the flanks of the steep hillside. With regular

Ross's Camp

Muncaster Fell rising above Eskdale Green

upright stones marking the edge it is a lasting tribute to the skill of the Roman engineers. The way leads down to intercept a grassy track. Bear right and continue to pass Muncaster Head farm and intercept a larger track. Turn right and follow the lane beneath the foot of the fell. On the left a sign marks 'Roman Tile Kilns' which are protected as a monument of national importance. It looks unimpressive, though nearby can be found heaps of baked clay bricks (please don't touch them). Mindboggling to think that they are almost 2,000 years old.

Pass the buildings of High Eskholme, and an intriguing stand of ancient yews, before the path breaks from the lane to ascend to the right. Beyond the row of cottages to the left, stands the remarkable octagonal 'Henry's Tower' (monument) where Henry VI was found (I wonder if they missed him) after the battle of Hexham in 1464. With the wall to the left continue rising with the path, up through the woods of Chapel Hill, until a section of open path leads to intercept the original track by the rhododendrons of Muncaster Tarn.

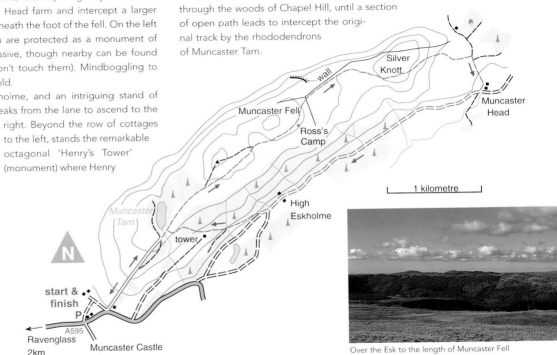

Henry's Tower

Over the Esk to the length of Muncaster Fell

WALK 64 FACT FILE

LENGTH: 11KM
TIME: 3½ HOURS
DIFFICULTY: DIFFICULT; WELL-DEFINED TRACK THOUGH BOGGY IN PLACES

START & FINISH: CAR PARK OPPOSITE ENTRANCE TO MUNCASTER CASTLE (098 967)
MAPS: OS L96 OR OL6

ACCESS: TAKE THE A595 S FROM EGREMONT
WATERING HOLES: MUNCASTER CASTLE GATEHOUSE INFORMATION CENTRE

BY WAST WATER BENEATH THE WASDALE SCREES

Forest Bridge, Easthwaite Farm, Wast Water, Lund Bridge, Low Wood, Wasdale Hall, Greendale, Roan Wood, Ashness How

INTRODUCTION

10KM SE OF EGREMONT. OVERLOOKED BY THE IMPOSING MASS OF WASDALE SCREES, THE COUNTRYSIDE AROUND THE FOOT OF WAST WATER, THE SOURCE OF THE RIVER IRT, PROVIDES A GLORIOUS MIX OF MOUNTAIN, FIELD, WOOD AND HILL. CROSSING AND RECROSSING THE RIVER IRT TO TRAVERSE THE LAKESHORE, THIS ANTICLOCKWISE CIRCUIT CONTINUES TO MAKE A REVEALING EXPLORATION OF THE REGION.

The magnificent mountain view up Wast Water

STEP BY STEP

▶ Cross the River Irt, once prized for its freshwater pearls, by Forest Bridge to take the track which leads off left to Easthwaite Farm. Pass the farm then take the path that leads right off the main track. Continue until the path bears right. Make a short ascent by the wall, before an exit left onto the open fellside. Wonderful views over the foot of Wast Water and along its length to Great Gable.

▶ Follow the path left in descent to gain a grassy track, and bear right to gain the bank of the River Irt which issues from the lake. Go left along the bank and then go right across Lund Bridge. Turn right. Follow the path

By Easthwaite Farm

through Low Wood to skirt the foot of Wast Water. Continue to pass a boathouse and on, until spacious views are revealed along the full length of the lake. Pass in front of Wasdale Hall, now a Youth Hostel. A plaque reads 'This Youth Hostel is one of many, both in this country and abroad, where young people, regardless of race or creed, may spend the night'. Looking out over the lake to Wasdale Screes it would be hard to imagine a finer setting, a more handsome building or a nobler sentiment.

▶ Continue along the path above the waters edge, until a stone stile leads up to the surfaced road. Bear right, follow the road to a junction, then turn left. Continue to cross over Greendale Bridge and then go left along the bridleway to pass through Roan Wood.

Bearing right, the track traverses the fields to ascend the open hillside of Ashness How. Descend the hill and keep straight on in the same direction. Follow the lane to bear left, past great beech trees, and emerge onto the surfaced road. Turn right and then left at the first junction.

Fell pony above Wast Water

Haymaking with Wasdale Screes beyond

Wast Water from Wasdale Hall point

1 kilometre

N

Greendale

Roan Wood

Ashness How

Woodhow Tarn

WAST WATER

Low Wood

Lund Bridge

Nether Wasdale

start & finish

River Irt

Forest Bridge

Easthwaite

WALK 65 FACT FILE

LENGTH: 8KM
TIME: 2¾ HOURS
DIFFICULTY: MODERATE; UNDULATING ASCENT AND DESCENT
START & FINISH: PARKING GROUND

SITED BETWEEN CINDERFIELD BRIDGE AND FOREST BRIDGE (129 038)
MAPS: OS L89 OR OL6
ACCESS: TAKE THE A595 S FROM EGREMONT TO TURN OFF THROUGH

GOSFORTH AND FOLLOW THE ROAD LEFT TO NETHER WASDALE
WATERING HOLES: NONE EN ROUTE, NEAREST ARE THE STRANDS AND THE SCREES IN NETHER WASDALE

THE ROUND OF ENNERDALE WATER

Bowness Plantation, Ennerdale Water, Char Dub Bridge, The Side Wood, Anglers' Crag

INTRODUCTION

17KM N OF EGREMONT. AT THE NW EDGE OF THE NATIONAL PARK, ENNERDALE WATER FORMS THE WATERY FOOT OF A DEEP MOUNTAIN VALLEY. WITH FINE VIEWS TO THE HIGH MOUNTAINS THIS CLOCKWISE CIRCUMNAVIGATION REVEALS THE MANY FACETS OF THIS QUIETLY IMPOSING LAKE.

INTRODUCTION

STEP BY STEP

▶ Bear left along the track beneath the forest and pass a finger peninsula which, bedecked with Scots Pine, frames the distant mountains of Steeple and Pillar beautifully. Keep along the track to the end of the lake. At this point a little path passes through a gap in the wall to the right and may be followed along the river bank to Char Dub Bridge.

▶ Char, an arctic species of fish, still spawn in the deep mint waters of Char Dub below the bridge. Cross the bridge and continue along the broad track towards the forest opposite. Before the track enters the trees take the ladder stile over the wall to the right and follow the path across the fields to regain the edge of the lake. The path, via a stile over the fence, leads into the sessile oak and deciduous woods of The Side. A flat circular area represents an ancient charcoal burner's ring. Beyond the woods the fellside becomes open and the steep craggy knoll of Anglers' Crag nears.

▶ Take the path which rises steeply to the top of the scree, to pass through the slag of an old iron bloomery site and with the levels of abandoned iron mines above. Follow the path rightwards to traverse around the craggy corner of the face. Though exposed and a little scrambly in places, the going isn't too difficult. As the path begins to descend, a 5m section of slabby rock presents

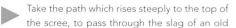
Char Dub Bridge

Over Ennerdale Water from the site of the former Angler's Inn

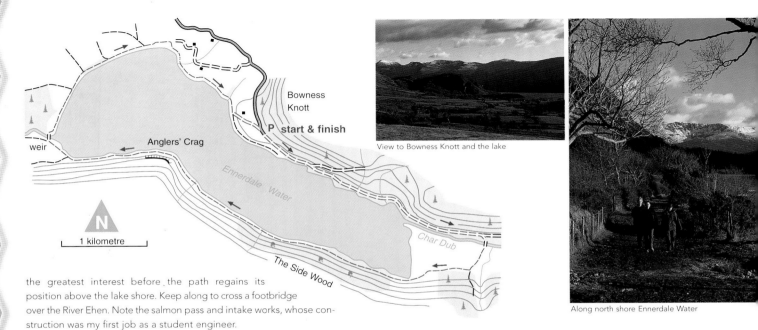

View to Bowness Knott and the lake

Along north shore Ennerdale Water

the greatest interest before the path regains its position above the lake shore. Keep along to cross a footbridge over the River Ehen. Note the salmon pass and intake works, whose construction was my first job as a student engineer.

▶ The going is easy, and views up the length of the lake quite superb. Opposite the wood a concrete and stone jetty mark the site of the former Angler's Inn — dismantled by the water authority in anticipation of raising the level of the lake. Fortunately the water was not raised. Follow the path, which runs mainly by the waters edge, until, with Bowness Knott rising to the left and a knoll in front, a little lane leads left back to the car park.

WALK 66 FACT FILE

LENGTH: 11KM
TIME: 3 HOURS
DIFFICULTY: MODERATE; EXPOSED WITH A LITTLE SCRAMBLE SECTION AROUND ANGLERS' CRAG
START & FINISH: CAR PARK BELOW BOWNESS KNOTT AT THE END OF THE PUBLIC ROAD (110 153)
MAPS: OS L89 OR OL4
ACCESS: N OF EGREMONT TAKE THE A5086 TO CLEATOR MOOR, THEN THE MINOR ROAD TO ENNERDALE BRIDGE. GO RIGHT AND KEEP RIGHT ON A MINOR ROAD FOLLOWING IT TO ITS TERMINUS BELOW BOWNESS KNOTT
WATERING HOLES: NONE EN ROUTE, FOX AND HOUNDS AND SHEPHERDS ARMS AT ENNERDALE BRIDGE

THROUGH LANTHWAITE WOOD BY THE FOOT OF CRUMMOCK WATER

Scalehill Bridge, River Cocker, Crummock Water, Boathouse, Lanthwaite Wood

11KM S OF COCKERMOUTH. AT THE HEAD OF LORTON VALE, LANTHWAITE WOOD ADORNS THE FOOT OF CRUMMOCK WATER ABOVE ISSUE OF THE RIVER COCKER. THIS SIMPLE ROUND OFFERS TREE-CLAD RIVERBANK, UNFORGETTABLE MOUNTAIN VIEWS OVER CRUMMOCK WATER AND MIXED WOODS.

STEP BY STEP

▶ Take the gate to leave the car park then immediately bear right to follow the wooded riverbank above the River Cocker. A most charming environment, though the going is a little rough in places. Those preferring easier walking, or perhaps by necessity in times of flood, may stick to the track.

▶ At the foot of Crummock Water bear left, passing a magnificent Scots Pine, to follow the track above the lake. The exceptional mountain vista includes Melbreak, Red Pike, High Stile and Grasmoor. Above the boathouse a path breaks off left up through the wood. Follow the path to

Lanthwaite Wood and Grasmoor rise above Crummock Water

Wooded path by River Cocker

make a curving route which rises to intercept a wide track. En route, near a stream, notice the slag of an ancient iron bloomery.

▶ Go left and follow the track in descent, excellent view back to Red Pike where the conifers have been felled, all the way back to the car park at the start.

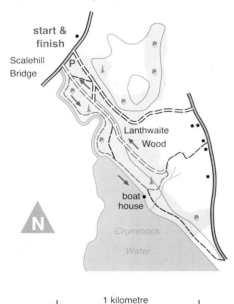

Scots pine by lake shore

View up the lake

The foot of Crummock Water

WALK 67 FACT FILE

LENGTH: 2.5KM
TIME: 1¼ HOURS
DIFFICULTY: EASY; STEEPISH ASCENT, GENTLE DESCENT

START & FINISH: SCALEHILL BRIDGE CAR PARK (149 215)
MAPS: OS L89 OR OL4
ACCESS: FOLLOW THE B5289 S FROM

COCKERMOUTH TO TURN RIGHT TOWARDS LOWESWATER
WATERING HOLES: NONE EN ROUTE, KIRKSTILE INN AT NEARBY LOWESWATER

A ROUND OF THE NEWLANDS VALLEY

Goldscope, Low Snab, Scope Beck, Low High Snab, Gillbrow, Rowling End Farm, Ghyll Bank, Skelgill, Little Town

INTRODUCTION

8KM SW OF KESWICK. ONCE THE HUB OF EXTENSIVE MINING ACTIVITY, THE CHARMING, NOW QUIET, NEWLANDS NESTLES DEEP IN THE NORTH WESTERN FELLS BETWEEN BUTTERMERE AND BORROWDALE. THIS CLOCKWISE ROUTE, TRAVERSING ITS THREE HEADS AND CROSSING THE BODY OF THE VALLEY, FULLY SAVOURS THE MAGICAL MOUNTAIN ATMOSPHERE.

STEP BY STEP

▶ Ascend the road in the direction of Little Town then bear right over the stile and up the steps to gain the track which leads to the first mountain head of the valley. Bear right, and continue along the track until, at the end of the stone wall a path goes right to cross a foot-bridge over Newlands Beck. The extensive tips of mine spoil are those of Goldscope Mine. In Elizabethan times sufficient gold was extracted from the copper for the mine to be claimed as Crown Property by Elizabeth.

▶ Bear left above Low Snab Farm and keep left to follow around beneath the heights of Scope End. Rise, to pass an old mine entrance and continue, until the stone wall below falls directly to Scope Beck. Descend by the wall,

Footbridge below Goldscope

boggy in places, to cross the narrow beck and rise to the track on the opposite side of the valley. Bear right and pass the dichotomously named cottages of Low High Snab to follow the road down the hill. Pass the first

Over Newlands Valley to Little Town

A view to Newlands Chapel

Fine chestnut by Skelgill

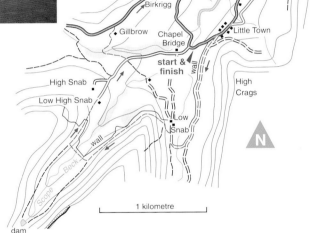

signed 'Public Footpath' to the left and take the second.

▶ Follow the track to enter the wood and cross a footbridge over Keskadale Beck. Rise to pass Gillbrow Farm and gain a road. Turn right keeping on the high road to cross Rigg Beck and descend to pass above Emerald Bank, until a little gate on the right leads, past Rowling End Farm, down to a footbridge over Newlands Beck and up to the road by Ghyll Bank. Turn left and then take the footpath which leads off to the right. Cross the fields to Skelgill. Go right, up the road, then right again through the buildings.

▶ A grassy path leads through the fields, an old trackway with wonderful views to the surrounding fells, to emerge once again onto a surfaced road. Turn left and pass through Little Town, the fabled home of Beatrix Potter's Lucie and Mrs Tiggywinkle, to descend the hill to Church Bridge.

WALK 68 FACT FILE

LENGTH: 8.5km

TIME: 2½ hours

DIFFICULTY: Moderate; boggy in places and includes a little river crossing over Scope Beck

START & FINISH: Limited parking by Chapel Bridge below Little Town (232 194)

MAPS: OS L89 or OL4

ACCESS: Briefly follow the A66 W from Keswick to turn off through Portinscale. Continue through Swinside to turn left by the bridge in Stair to pass through Little Town

WATERING HOLES: None en route, Swinside Inn nearby

SEATHWAITE TO STYHEAD TARN VIA TAYLORGILL FORCE

Taylorgill Force, Styhead Gill, Styhead Tarn, Sty Head, Stockley Bridge

14KM S OF KESWICK. RISING TO THE HIGH COL BETWEEN GREAT GABLE AND SCAFELL'S GREAT END, THE STYHEAD PASS BETWEEN BORROWDALE AND WASDALE ONCE SERVED AS AN IMPORTANT PACKHORSE ROUTE TO THE WEST COAST. THIS ROUTE ASCENDS VIA THE IMPRESSIVE WATERFALL OF TAYLORGILL FORCE TO RETURN BY STOCKLEY BRIDGE OVER GRAINS GILL.

Styhead Tarn

STEP BY STEP

▶ A short walk into a wonderfully wild mountain world. Enter the farmyard then take the passageway through the building to the right to cross the footbridge over Seathwaite Beck just above its confluence with Sourmilk Gill. Immediately go left, taking the little gate through the stone wall. Follow the path which rises through the fields above the west bank of the beck. As the going steepens scrambly ascent leads to a little gate, beyond which there is a view across to Taylorgill Force. The waterfall, particularly impressive in times of spate, falls clear for some 30m down the ravine of Styhead Gill.

▶ Beyond the gate the path rises with a little exposed section of rocky scrambling before continuing more easily. Pass the pines and continue by the delightful open banks and rock slides of Styhead Gill. The going levels to pass the archetypal mountain tarn – Styhead Tarn. A little rise, passing the Mountain Rescue Box, leads to the top of a rock crest and the summit of the pass. A view into

The impressive waterfall of Taylorgill Force

the head of Wasdale.

▶   Return to pass the tarn and on to cross the beck by a wooden footbridge. Follow the stony track above the true right bank of Styhead Gill, descending to pass the pines and on down through a gate to the stone arched pack-horse bridge of Stockley Bridge over Grains Gill. Follow the track back to the welcoming portals of Seathwaite Farm.

Stone-arched Stockley Bridge

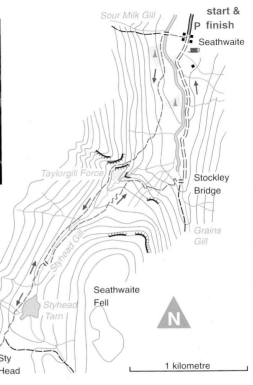

Styhead Gill

A view over the path to Seathwaite below

WALK 69 FACT FILE

LENGTH: 7.5KM

TIME: 2 HOURS

DIFFICULTY: DIFFICULT; A SHORT SECTION OF SCRAMBLY ASCENT TO PASS THE WATERFALL

START & FINISH: BELOW THE FARM AT THE HEAD OF SEATHWAITE (236 122)

MAPS: OS L89 OR OL4

ACCESS: FOLLOW THE BORROWDALE ROAD FROM KESWICK TURNING LEFT AT

SEATOLLER TO SEATHWAITE

WATERING HOLES: CAFE AT SEATHWAITE FARM

STONETHWAITE TO LANGSTRATH BY TWA BECKS

Alisongrass Hoghouse Wood, Galleny Force, Smithymire Island, Johnny House, Stonethwaite Bridge

INTRODUCTION

11KM S OF KESWICK. UNDER THE RUGGED
INFLUENCE OF HIGH FELLS AND STEEP CRAGS, THE
HAMLET OF STONETHWAITE NESTLES WITHIN THE
EASTERN HEAD OF THE TWIN HEADS OF BORROWDALE.
THIS DELIGHTFUL ROUND FOLLOWS BY STONETHWAITE
BECK TO CROSS BY FOOTBRIDGE ITS TWO FEEDER
STREAMS: LANGSTRATH BECK AND GREENUP GILL.

INTRODUCTION

STEP BY STEP

▶ An extended title to this walk could be 'Stonethwaite to Langstrath by twa (two) becks, and return crossing yan (one) gill (Greenup)'. The considerable heaps of stones washed from the mountains to form the banks and riverbed of Stonethwaite Beck, give rise to the name Stone-thwaite; thwaite being Old Norse (Viking), for a clearing. Langstrath Beck in particular, whose confluence with Greenup Gill forms Stonethwaite Beck, is noted for its deep clear pools, tumbling waterfalls and great rock slides. A delectable walk of mixed woods and heady mountain ambience.

Rocky slides, Langstrath Beck

▶ Take the right lane which leads from the centre of the hamlet and keep along the stony track to pass by Bull Crag and Alisongrass Hoghouse woods. Pass a climbing hut, stone barn, and continue along the walled lane until, at a polished boulder, open ground lies to the left. Bearing right leads directly to the lane to follow the west bank of Langstrath Beck. More interestingly bear left to a rougher path above the rockpools and waterfalls of Stonethwaite Beck and on to pass Galleny Force. Keep along the riverbank, over a rocky channel, onto Smithymire Island, above the confluence of Greenup Gill and Langstrath Beck. Directly below, a great deep green pool is fed by the tumbling fall of

Stonethwaite Beck with mighty Eagle Crag rising above

Smithymire Force. Above the island and its stand of oaks, long rock slides and cascading waters make this a delightful location. The thick red deposits on the island, the iron bloom found in the river banks above, along with the name Smithymire, show this to be an ancient site of iron manufacture. Re-cross the rock channel and ascend the open brackened ground beyond the river to regain the track which leads up into Langstrath.

▶ Ascend the walled track to start along the long wild, mountain valley of Langstrath until, passing the remains of Johnny House over the wall to the right, a wooden footbridge leads left across Langstrath Beck. Turn left, following the path along the bank of the beck, to descend by the falls. The massive bastion of Eagle Crag towers above. Cross the wooden footbridge over Greenup Gill.

▶ Intercept the track and go left, with the waterfall of Gallen Force amongst the trees down to the left. Continue by wood and field to find the stone arched Stonethwaite Bridge to the left.

Smithymire Island on true left of beck

Stonethwaite Bridge

Stonethwaite

start & finish

Stonethwaite Beck

campsite

Galleny Force

Alisongrass Hoghouse Wood

N

Johnny House

Langstrath Beck

Green Gill

Johnny House footbridge over Langstrath Beck

WALK 70 FACT FILE

LENGTH: 4KM
TIME: 1½ HOURS
DIFFICULTY: EASY; GOODS TRACKS AND PATH OFTEN WET IN PLACES
START & FINISH: BORROWDALE'S

STONETHWAITE (262 138)
MAPS: OS L89 OR OL4
ACCESS: FOLLOW THE BORROWDALE ROAD S FROM KESWICK TURNING LEFT, BEYOND ROSTHWAITE, TO STONETHWAITE

WATERING HOLES: CAFE AND LANGSTRATH COUNTRY INN AT STONETHWAITE

BORROWDALE'S BOWDERSTONE TO WATENDLATH

Bowderstone, Birkett's Leap, Watendlath, Lodore Falls, Grange

7.5KM S OF KESWICK. BEYOND DERWENT WATER, BORROWDALE SQUEEZES THROUGH THE 'JAWS OF BORROWDALE', ABOVE WHICH AND BEHIND GRANGE FELL, LIES THE REMOTE MOUNTAIN HAMLET WATENDLATH. MAKING AN ANTICLOCKWISE CIRCUIT AROUND GRANGE FELL THIS WALK CONTRASTS THE EXQUISITE LAKE AND WOOD WITH THE UNTAMED CRAG AND FELL.

STEP BY STEP

▶ Here in reality is the fictional world of Rogue Harris and Judith Paris so evocatively portrayed by Hugh Walpole in his series of novels. The fine oakwoods fringe Derwent Water's expansive mirror of light. The jagged crags and huge boulders provide backdrop to the quaint cottages and remote farms, to the hamlet of Watendlath, a mountain tarn and the tumbling falls of Lodore. Below the car park take the low track to pass the bottom slate quarry and continue to pass the huge boulder of the Bowderstone. Most probably tumbled from the crags above it is much loved by rock climbers. There is also an easy wooden ladder to the top. Remarkably its two thousand ton bulk rests balanced on a long edge, it vaguely resembles a rhomboid set on its edge, and you can shake hands through a hole beneath it. In Swedish, 'Bowderstein' means 'balanced rock'.

▶ The track descends to the road. Go left along the road until, on the left, around the bend of Red Brow, a gate at the back of a little parking area opens onto a track. Take the high track, Public Bridleway to Watendlath, generally bearing right to make diagonal ascent of the hillside. Intercept a track which rises from Rosthwaite, and climb directly to pass Birkett's Leap and on over Grange fell via Puddingstone Bank, before falling to Watendlath (home of Judith Paris).

The Bowderstone – 'balanced rock'

Over the head of Derwent Water to the 'Jaws of Borrowdale'

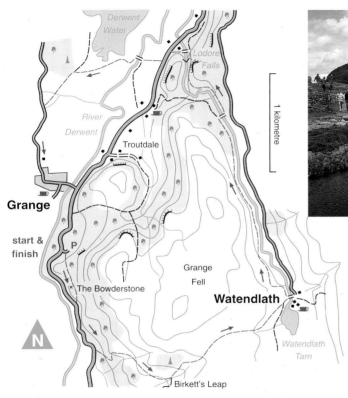

Grange

start & finish

P

The Bowderstone

Troutdale

Derwent Water

Lodore Falls

River Derwent

1 kilometre

Grange Fell

Watendlath

Watendlath Tarn

Birkett's Leap

N

Packhorse Bridge, Watendlath

Char fishing on Derwent Water

▶ From the hamlet follow down the left side of the beck descending the valley until a footbridge crosses to the right to enter Lodore Woods. Bear left and follow the stony path/track down by the side of the beck to pass the myriad tumbling waterfalls of Lodore Falls. A footbridge leads left across the beck and behind the Lodore Hotel to gain the Borrowdale road.

▶ Turn left until, beneath Shepherd's Crag, a path bears off right to cross the fields and a footbridge over the River Derwent. Continue on to a surfaced road. Go left to Grange and on over the multi-arched stone bridge. Turn right along the road back to the car park.

WALK 71 FACT FILE

LENGTH: 10KM

TIME: 3 HOURS

DIFFICULTY: DIFFICULT; MILDLY STRENUOUS ASCENT AND DESCENT, GOOD

PATHS PREVAIL

START & FINISH: QUAYFOOT QUARRY CAR PARK (253 168)

MAPS: OS L89 OR OL4

ACCESS: PROCEED S DOWN THE BORROWDALE ROAD FROM KESWICK

WATERING HOLES: CAFES AT WATENDLATH AND GRANGE

OVER CAT BELLS RETURNING BY DERWENT WATER

Skelgill Bank, Cat Bells, Hause Gate, Manesty Wood, Brandelhow Wood

6KM SW OF KESWICK. THE HIGH GRACEFUL SHOULDER OF CAT BELLS FLANKS THE WESTERN EDGE OF SPARKLING DERWENT WATER. OFFERING WONDERFUL POSITION AND OUTSTANDING VIEWS THIS ANTICLOCKWISE ROUND TRAVERSES SKELGILL BANK AND CAT BELLS FROM HAWES END TO MAKE RETURN BY THE WOODED SHORES OF THE LAKE.

STEP BY STEP

▶ Take the stone steps which rise from the car park, and follow the well-worn path, over littered fragments and polished outcrops of grey Skiddaw Slate, to make steep ascent of Skelgill Bank. Continue along the level ridge, to cross the workings of the ancient Brandelhow copper mine which has risen all the way from the lake shore far below. The ridge dips down to a col beneath the final pyramid of Cat Bells. Make steep ascent to gain the polished rock dome summit of Cat Bells and enjoy the superb and extensive view; particularly outstanding over the Newlands valley to the North Western Fells and over Derwent Water and its emerald isles to Skiddaw and Blencathra beyond Keswick.

Path rising from Skelgill Bank

▶ Continue along the shoulder, making descent to Hause Gate before a path leads off down to the left. Descend the path, with a steep awkward rock section near the top, handrail in situ, before the going eases. Follow the path rightwards, diagonally down the hillside until, at an acute bend, with the main path heading off to the left, a path to the right is followed and will be found to lead down to the surfaced road. Bear left until a gate/kissing gate on the right, leads into Manesty Woods. Follow a surfaced

Over Derwent Water to Cat Bells

track until the lake can be seen. A route leads off right to the lakeshore at Myrtle Bay. Take this then bear left through the mixed woods and follow the path/track, keeping to the lakeshore whenever possible, to pass; Abbots Bay, Brandelhow Point with its fine house, Brandelhow Bay and its banks of mine spoil, Brandelhow Woods, Withesike Bay, Victoria Bay and Otterbield Bay. The path/track then bears away from the lake to pass beneath the buildings of Hawes End Outdoor Pursuits Centre to intercept a steeply rising track. Turn left and follow the track back to the road and on over the cattle grid.

Over Abbot's Bay to Brandlehow Point

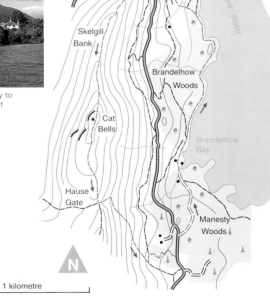

North from the shore of Derwent Water (Withesike Bay) to distant Blencathra

1 kilometre

WALK 72 FACT FILE

LENGTH: 7KM
TIME: 2½ HOURS
DIFFICULTY: DIFFICULT; STRENUOUS ASCENT AND A SHORT SECTION OF SCRAMBLY DESCENT

START & FINISH: HAWES END CAR PARK (247 212)
MAPS: OS L89 OR OL4
ACCESS: FROM KESWICK FOLLOW THE A66 W TO PORTINSCALE. PROCEED TO

SWINDALE, TURNING LEFT BEFORE THE HAMLET, AND RISE TO GAIN THE CAR PARK OF HAWES END
WATERING HOLES: NONE EN ROUTE, SWINSIDE INN NEARBY

KESWICK'S GRETA GORGE

Fitz Park, Keswick Old Station, Windebrowe, Brundholme Woods, Brundholme, Old Railway

INTRODUCTION

KESWICK. BELOW LATRIGG THE RIVER GRETA FOLLOWS A TORTUOUS PATH THROUGH A HEAVILY WOODED GORGE. THIS ROUTE ASCENDS THE GORGE, TRAVERSING THROUGH BRUNDHOLME WOODS WHICH BEDECK ITS NORTHERN SLOPES, BEFORE DESCENDING TO MAKE EASY RETURN ALONG THE OLD RAILWAY LINE.

INTRODUCTION

STEP BY STEP

▶ The fine trees, horse chestnut, limes, oak and sycamore, of Fitz Park make a pleasurable start to this rewarding walk. Cross the A5271, the main road through the town, and bear left to find a footbridge into the park. Bear right and leave the park taking the steps near the Museum. Turn left along the road and left again to cross in front of the swimming pool. Pass the end of the pool to enter the old station car park.

▶ Turn right until, a little way along the old platform, an opening leads off down to the left. Go right and find a narrow stile leading onto the road. Proceed down the road until, just before the old railway bridge, a road branches off left (signed 'Public Footpath Windebrowe'). Follow this through the trees and go left at the next junction. Exit through the gate of Brundholme Country House Hotel and bear right to follow the road over Windebrowe.

The Greta through Brundholme Woods

Where the Greta flows through Keswick

Old railway return

Autumn colours

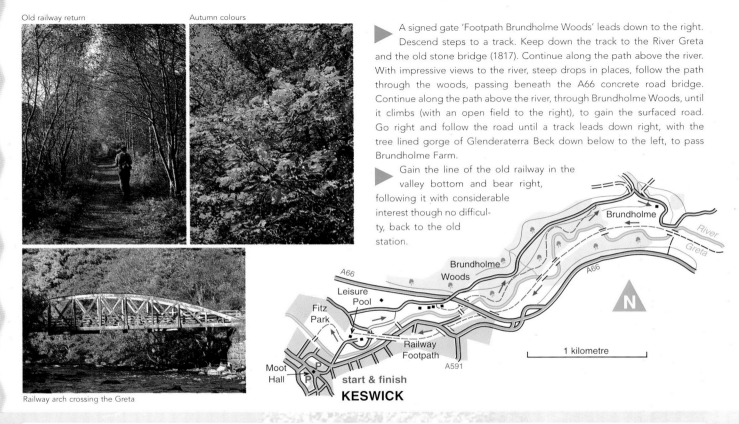

Railway arch crossing the Greta

A signed gate 'Footpath Brundholme Woods' leads down to the right. Descend steps to a track. Keep down the track to the River Greta and the old stone bridge (1817). Continue along the path above the river. With impressive views to the river, steep drops in places, follow the path through the woods, passing beneath the A66 concrete road bridge. Continue along the path above the river, through Brundholme Woods, until it climbs (with an open field to the right), to gain the surfaced road. Go right and follow the road until a track leads down right, with the tree lined gorge of Glenderaterra Beck down below to the left, to pass Brundholme Farm.

Gain the line of the old railway in the valley bottom and bear right, following it with considerable interest though no difficulty, back to the old station.

Brundholme

Brundholme Woods

Leisure Pool

Fitz Park

Railway Footpath

River Greta

A66

A66

A591

N

1 kilometre

Moot Hall

start & finish

KESWICK

WALK 73 FACT FILE

LENGTH: 7.5KM
TIME: 2½ HOURS
DIFFICULTY: MODERATE; AN UNDULATING JOURNEY UPSTREAM, LEVEL

RETURN
START & FINISH: KESWICK (266 235)
MAPS: OS L89 OR OL4
ACCESS: CAR PARKS ARE FOUND S AND

N OF THE MOOT HALL AND KESWICK'S MAIN STREET
WATERING HOLES: PLENTIFUL IN KESWICK

BY THIRLMERE'S SHORE TO CASTLE ROCK

Thirlmere Shore, Greathow Wood, Thirlmere Dam, Legburthwaite, Castle Rock, Stanah

INTRODUCTION

16KM N OF AMBLESIDE. WHILST THE EXPANSE OF THIRLMERE RESERVOIR AND ITS SWATHE OF CONIFERS DOMINATE THIS VALLEY THERE IS NEVERTHELESS MUCH OF INTEREST TO BE DISCOVERED. THIS CLOCKWISE ROUND FOLLOWS BY THE SHORE OF THE RESERVOIR BEFORE ROUNDING GREAT HOW AND PASSING BENEATH CASTLE ROCK TO MAKE HIGH RETURN.

The sheer walls of Castle Rock

STEP BY STEP

▶ Thirlmere Reservoir was inundated by Manchester Corporation in 1894. Take the path below the car park to bear left across the flank of the hill. The first surprise is the sudden appearance, fenced in the trees, of a waterfall feeding a busy stream which falls to the reservoir. The water originated from a water leat, to be followed on return, which traverses the hillside far above. Descend to the woods above the shore and bear right along the waymarked path. Cross the little footbridge, by the old iron boat rails, in front of Dalehead Hall, and rise through the woods to intercept a track. After a little way the path rises to the right and offers a view through the fine beech trees to The Dodds. Briefly join a track, then bear left and take the low path which traverses the steep flanks of Great How above the shore.

Across Thirlmere to the east shore

▶ Descend stone steps to gain the road at the end of the dam. Bear right and on to cross the main road and follow up the old road until a kissing gate on the right leads into the Legburthwaite car park. A narrow path, opposite the toilets, leads to the road.

Cross here and ascend the steps opposite. Climb the grassy path to intercept a track. The great bastion of Castle Rock, a favourite rock climbing crag, stands above. My father made the first ascent of its North Face in 1939 by a route known as Overhanging Bastion – a testpiece of its day.

▶ Cross the track and make steep ascent with a little plantation to the right. The feint path joins the water leat. Stone steps lead over the wall to the right. Continue to follow the water leat by its right side, narrow in places and care must be taken. Wooden stiles facilitate the crossing of barriers. Above the buildings of Stannah a track is intercepted – this is the Sticks Pass high mountain route to Glenridding. Follow it briefly, to cross the wooden footbridge over the rift of Stanah Gill, then bear right to follow the path above the wall. This leads on to pass, via a footbridge, the waterfalls of Fisherplace Gill. Don't take the path which descends to Thirlspot but keep on to make gradual descent to intercept the Helvellyn path. A swing right leads into the large car park on the east side of the A591.

Thirlmere Dam, completed 1894

Along east shore of Thirlmere

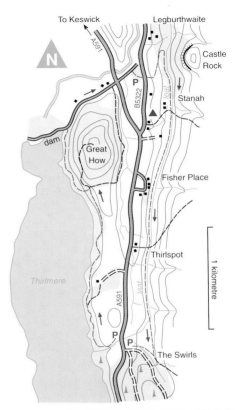

WALK 74 FACT FILE

LENGTH: 7KM
TIME: 2½ HOURS
DIFFICULTY: MODERATE; ROUGH GOING IN PLACES

START & FINISH: CAR PARK BY A591 OVERLOOKING THIRLMERE RESERVOIR (315 170)
MAPS: OS L90 OR OL5

ACCESS: FOLLOW THE A591 N FROM AMBLESIDE
WATERING HOLES: NONE EN ROUTE, KING'S HEAD INN AT NEARBY THIRLSPOT

BY BASSENTHWAITE LAKE AND ST BEGA'S

Watches, High Side, Mire Side, Scarness, Bassenthwaite Lake, St Bega's, Mirehouse

16KM N OF KESWICK. SQUEEZED BENEATH MIGHTY SKIDDAW AND THE NORTH WESTERN FELLS BASSENTHWAITE LAKE IS THE MOST NORTHERLY OF THE MAJOR LAKES. THIS ROUND ABOVE AND ALONG ITS EASTERN SHORE, TRAVERSING THE FLANKS OF ULLOCK PIKE AND RETURNING BY ST BEGA'S OFFERS A WEALTH OF DRAMATIC SCENERY.

STEP BY STEP

▶ Cross the footbridge above the tea room and go first left and then right to ascend a grassy track through the tall pines. Turn left along the high track. It narrows and drops to intercept a track rising from below. Keep right and make steep ascent to gain the open fell, then go left to traverse above the fell wall, fairly level, before rising slightly to round the nose of Watches.

▶ Fall to intercept a track and turn left to follow the track and grassy path to the left (signed) over a ladder stile and down through the fields. Continue to join a path and go left to emerge onto the surfaced road. Turn left until, at the bottom of the hill and junction with A591, a signed path directly opposite the buildings of High Side is taken. Descend the field to its corner and bear right down the centre of a long narrow field to continue through fields to the buildings of Mire Side. Go left between the buildings and exit to the right (signed Scarness). Follow across the field (ill-defined path) with a hedge to the right. Exit onto a road and cross it to a cattle grid and

Fellside below Watches

concrete track opposite. Follow down this and through the gate to enter the property of Scarness. Walk across the lawn (public footpath!) to the left of the house and join the drive to follow it leftward to exit onto the road.

Over Bassenthwaite Lake to the green meadows of the east shore

Turn left then right down an overgrown path to gain the lakeshore (National Nature Reserve). Follow the path round the headland between Scarness and Bowness Bay and continue to regain the road. Bear right along the tree lined road until, within a little wood, a (signed) path bears off to the right. Cross the fields, an ancient trackway, and little wood to gain the lane leading to St Bega's Church.

Go right, then follow the way off left before the church, to gain and follow a track leading to the right of Mirehouse. Whilst staying at Mirehouse, Tennyson took his inspiration to write 'Morte d'Arthur' – if you should wonder where the idea for the sword Excalibur arose, then you may find it on an ancient gravestone preserved within St Bega's (heed the notice 'Please close the door because of the swallows').

High track above the woods

The classic toadstool Fly agaric (poisonous)

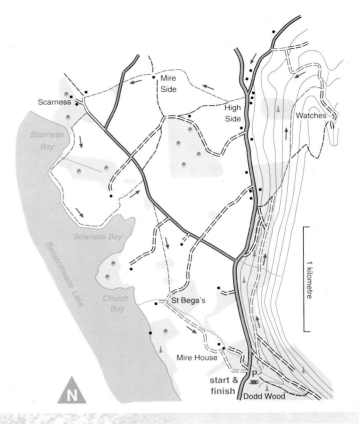

WALK 75 FACT FILE

LENGTH: 10.5KM
TIME: 3 HOURS
DIFFICULTY: DIFFICULT; SOME STRENUOUS ASCENT AND ROUGH GOING

START & FINISH: : DODD WOOD, OLD SAWMILL TEA ROOM CAR PARK OPPOSITE MIREHOUSE (235 281)
MAPS: OS L90 OR OL4

ACCESS: FOLLOW THE A591 BASSENTHWAITE ROAD FROM KESWICK
WATERING HOLES: OLD SAWMILL TEA ROOM

GLENDERAMACKIN AND SOUTHER FELL

Glenderamackin, White Horse Bent, Mouthwaite Combe Head, Souther Fell, Beckside

INTRODUCTION

15KM NE OF KESWICK. CUTTING THROUGH THE QUIET FORGOTTEN HILLS ON THE E EDGE OF THE NORTHERN FELLS THE LITTLE RIVER GLENDERAMACKIN LOOPS AROUND SOUTHER FELL THROUGH MUNGRISDALE. MAKING AN ANTICLOCKWISE CIRCUIT FROM MUNGRISDALE THIS ROUTE RISES THROUGH THE PLEASANTLY DESERTED RIVER VALLEY TO MAKE RETURN ALONG THE GENTLE SHOULDER OF SOUTHER FELL.

INTRODUCTION

STEP BY STEP

▶ Fashioned from the softer rocks of Skiddaw slate the generally smooth and rounded terrain of this mountain region is bereft of neither drama or an air of wild desolation. Long gradual ascent provides an easy way to climb this fell which offers expansive views over the plains of the Eden Valley. Head N up the road. Cross the bridge and on to the hairpin bend. Go left to leave the road, passing the telephone kiosk, and follow the track above the north bank of the river. Bear left and cross little Bullfell Beck by a footbridge.

▶ Keep along the track above River Glenderamackin to ford Bannerdale Beck. The dark crags of Skiddaw Slate, the combes and mines of Bannerdale Fell hang to the right. Round the shoulder of Bannerdale Fell, known as White Horse Bent. The easiest way is to keep climbing and cross the River Glenderamackin by

Footbridge over River Glenderamackin

the wooden footbridge on the left. Make diagonal ascent to the level shoulder above the head of Mousthwaite Comb.

▶ Bear left and make reasonably easy ascent of the long shoulder of Souther Fell (pronounced Sowter). Pass a large circular cairn topped

Souther Fell rises above Mungrisdale with the valley of Glenderamackin to the right

by a rock of white quartz and continue along the level shoulder heading north to a little rock knoll – the summit.

▶ Keep north and continue down the steepening nose of the fell to reach a stone wall near its base. Go right along the wall (no access straight on) continuing to gain a surfaced road. Boggy in places. Go left down the hill until at the bottom a grassy lane continues on down to the River Glenderamackin just upstream of the buildings of Beckside. Before reaching the ford, which crosses the river, steps on the right give access to a narrow footbridge. Cross this, then go left to exit the field via a squeeze stile. Go right climbing the bank to the road. Head upstream to regain the parking area at the start.

Crossing Bullfell Beck

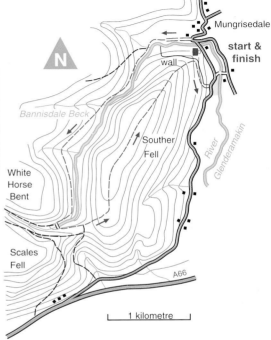

Cairn on Souther Fell

By Glenderamackin

WALK 76 FACT FILE

LENGTH: 9.5km
TIME: 2½ hours
DIFFICULTY: Difficult; straightforward ascent with steeper descent

START & FINISH: Mungrisdale, parking off the road above the river (364 301)
MAPS: OS L90 or OL5
ACCESS: Follow the A66 E from

Keswick continuing through Threlkeld and Scales to turn N along the minor road to Mungrisdale
WATERING HOLES: The Mill Inn at Mungrisdale

AIRA FORCE AND HIGH FORCE WATERFALLS

Aira Force, High Force, Dockray, Old Quarry

16KM SW OF PENRITH. AS AIRA BECK PASSES FROM DOCKRAY TO ULLSWATER IT TUMBLES THROUGH A NARROW WOODED RAVINE VIA THE DELIGHTFUL HIGH FORCE AND THE SPECTACULAR AIRA FORCE WATERFALLS. THIS ANTICLOCKWISE CIRCUIT PASSES AIRA FORCE AND HIGH FORCE VIA THEIR E BANK BEFORE CLIMBING TO DOCKRAY AND RETURNING TO THE RIVER BY THE W BANK.

STEP BY STEP

▶ Fine mixed woods, containing some magnificent ancient pine, plus the great 20m cascade of Aira Force, all fuse with the overall excellence of the surrounding countryside to make this a delightful outing.

▶ Leave the car park, beneath the arch, and cross the field until the path leads right into the woods. Go right over the footbridge to cross Aira Beck and continue to follow the terraced track. Take the low route to gain the impressive view of the fall of Aira Force from the bottom bridge before climbing to the upper narrow stone arched bridge via the steps and hand rails. A stomach-churning view down the falls and a slate memorial plaque to Cecil Spring Rice.

▶ Follow the path up the east bank (true left) of the beck. A short deviation may be made by descending to a footbridge crossing the beck (viewpoint). Return to the main path and continue to the delightful

Rainbows below Aira Force

High Force in spate

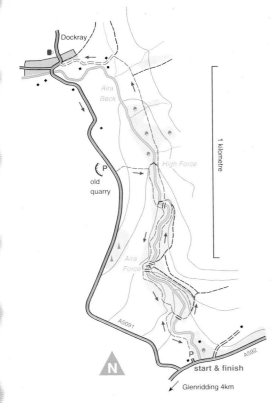

Dockray

Aira Beck

1 kilometre

P
old quarry

High Force

Aira Force

A5091

A592

N

start & finish

Glenridding 4km

High Force

rocky falls of High Force. Keep along the path and enter the little wood. Beyond the wood, fields lead easily to a junction of ways. Go left and enter Dockray directly opposite The Royal Hotel.

▶ Turn left down the road until, by the old quarry car park, a path leads off left (sign post 'Lower Pinetum'!). Go directly down the field and bear right to follow back down the west bank of the beck.

Beyond High Force

Signpost and The Royal Inn, Dockray

WALK 77 FACT FILE

LENGTH: 4.5km
TIME: 2 hours
DIFFICULTY: Moderate; ascend and descend on straightforward paths

START & FINISH: Aira Force car park (400 200) or if full the old quarry car park by the A5091 (397 210)
MAPS: OS L90 or OL5

ACCESS: From Penrith follow the A66 and then the A592 Ullswater road
WATERING HOLES: Cafe by the car park, The Royal Hotel in Dockray

UP GLENRIDDING AND DOWN GLENCOYNE TO ROUND SHEFFIELD PIKE

Greenside Lead Mine, Lucy's Tongue, Nick Head, Seldom Seen, Ullswater

15KM N OF AMBLESIDE. SEPARATED BY SHEFFIELD PIKE, ABOVE GLENRIDDING AT THE HEAD OF ULLSWATER, TWO CONTRASTING MOUNTAIN VALLEYS FALL TO THE LAKE. THIS ROUTE MAKES A CLOCKWISE CIRCUIT, RISING BY GLENRIDDING AND THE OLD GREENSIDE LEAD MINES AND FALLING BY GLENCOYNE AND THE COTTAGES OF SELDOM SEEN.

STEP BY STEP

▶ From the car park take the road which rises centrally through the houses of Glenridding. Rise with the road, don't turn off, until it levels and becomes surfaced. Pass the cottages and continue to follow the Greenside Road which runs above the Youth Hostel and on over the bridge into a cluster of former mine buildings. The workings, mine spoil tips, shafts and tunnels, are extensive. Greenside Lead Mine, worked into the early 1960's, was once the largest lead mine in England.

▶ Rise with the track, then bear right to ascend the zigzags. Round the hillside beneath the craggy slopes of Stang End, and pass the long flue of the lead smelting furnace chimney 'The Chimney' to climb Lucy's Tongue. Cross the footbridge and ascend the hillside to the right to gain the level col of Nick Head.

Over Ullswater to Sheffield Pike

Up Glenridding to Greenside Mine

Make diagonal descent rightwards, following the path down Bleabank Side to cross the slopes of Sheffield Pike. With excellent views down the length of Ullswater continue down to Glencoyne Woods. Pass the concealed row of cottages, Seldom Seen, down to the left, and continue along the track. Keep left to intercept the main road.

Go right, to follow the path beneath the road and beside the lake where possible, beneath Stybarrow Crag and back to Glenridding.

Seldom Seen cottages

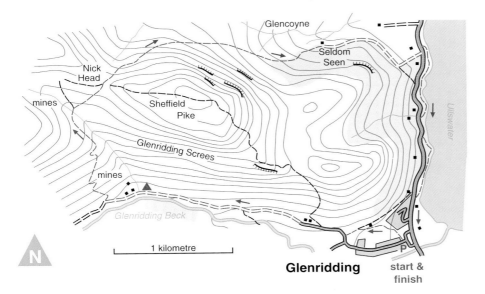
Glencoyne
Seldom Seen
Nick Head
mines
Sheffield Pike
Glenridding Screes
mines
Glenridding Beck
Ullswater

1 kilometre

N

Glenridding

start & finish

Down Ullswater from above Glencoyne

WALK 78 FACT FILE

LENGTH: 8km
TIME: 2½ hours
DIFFICULTY: Difficult; steep ascent, gentler descent
START & FINISH: Glenridding car

PARK (386 169)
MAPS: OS L90 or OL5
ACCESS: Take the Kirkstone Road. Rise steeply from Ambleside to cross the Kirkstone Pass and follow the

A592 directly to Glenridding
WATERING HOLES: Travellers Rest en route, plentiful in Glenridding

A CIRCUIT OF BROTHERS WATER

Brothers Water, Hartsop Hall, Ancient Settlement, Caudale Bridge, Horseman Bridge

10KM N OF AMBLESIDE. LOCATED AT THE NARROW HEAD OF THE LONG ULLSWATER VALLEY, LITTLE BROTHERS WATER'S DARK MIRROR REFLECTS MANY DIFFERENT MOODS. THIS SIMPLE CLOCKWISE CIRCUIT EXTENDS TO PASS THROUGH THE IMPRESSIVE ANCIENT SETTLEMENT WITHIN THE FORK BETWEEN DOVEDALE AND KIRKSTONEFOOT.

STEP BY STEP

▶ Follow the track through the wonderful oak woods above the western shore of the lake. Pass the interesting buildings of Hartsop Hall and bear right. Before the barns and outbuildings go left, to cross a little wooden sleeper bridge, to take a gate leading into the field.

▶ Follow the grassy track across the field and take the stone slab bridge over Dovedale Beck. Piles of stones, raised earthworks and huge boulders standing to a height of 2.5m mark a prehistoric site of some importance; set amidst dramatic mountain scenery. Continue along the grassy track to pass in front of a barn. Bear left to traverse above the wall. Follow the path until, as it begins to rise up to Scandale Pass, a lesser path breaks off to the left to cross little Caiston Beck by a footbridge.

▶ Bear first right (signed) then left through the gap in the wall to cross Kirkstone Beck via a little wooden sleeper bridge. An indefinite path leads across the boggy ground and up to gain the A592. Turn left along the road, grass verge, to cross Caudale Bridge and on to the Brotherswater Inn.

Ancient settlement beneath Dovedale

Lovely Brothers Water with Angletarn Pikes seen above

Bear left in front of the inn and then right at the junction, ascending until a permisssive path leads off left. Follow the path below the road and along the shore of the lake (can be flooded – if so ascend to the road) continuing across the meadows until forced out right onto the road once more. Go left and follow the pavement to cross Horseman Bridge and return to Cow Bridge.

Over the ancient settlement to Hartsop Hall and Brothers Water

Footbridge over Caiston Beck

North over Brothers Water

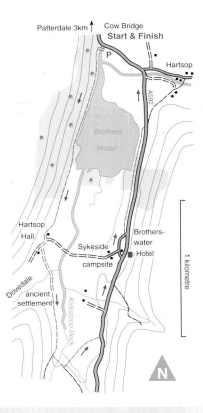

WALK 79 FACT FILE

LENGTH: 6KM

TIME: 1½ HOURS

DIFFICULTY: EASY, CAN BE BOGGY BENEATH THE KIRKSTONE PASS

START & FINISH: COW BRIDGE CAR PARK HARTSOP (402 134)

MAPS: OS L90 OR OL5

ACCESS: TAKE THE KIRKSTONE ROAD TO RISE STEEPLY FROM AMBLESIDE AND CROSS THE KIRKSTONE PASS. FOLLOW THE A592 DIRECTLY TO HARTSOP

WATERING HOLES: BROTHERSWATER INN EN ROUTE

MARDALE HEAD TO CASTLE CRAG

Mardale Head, The Rigg, Bowderthwaite Bridge, Randale Beck Bridge, Gate Crag, Castle Crag

INTRODUCTION

32KM SW OF PENRITH. WILD AND DESOLATE, FLOODED BY HAWESWATER RESERVOIR, THE HEAD OF MARDALE IS DOMINATED TO THE WEST BY HANGING CORRIES, A LONG RIDGE, AND A MOUNTAIN VALLEY, FALLING FROM THE GREAT SHOULDER OF HIGH STREET. THIS LINEAR ROUTE TRAVERSES ABOVE THE WESTERN SHORELINE TO ROUND THE RIGG, CROSS BOWDERTHWAITE BRIDGE AND VISIT CASTLE CRAG BEFORE MAKING RETURN.

STEP BY STEP

▶ Take the track from the head of the road and bear off right, following the line of the wall, to take the footbridge over Mardale Beck. Take the stony path traversing the hillside above the reservoir. Contour above the conifers to cross the foot of the ridge known as The Rigg.

▶ Descend to enter an avenue of little standing stones. Cross a tiny footbridge and enter a larch plantation. Leave the trees and follow down the avenue of stones to Bowderthwaite Bridge. Cross the wooden footbridge and continue to cross the stone arch packhorse bridge over Randale Beck. Continue below the trees, with a worthy view east from the top of Gate Crag, and keep along the path until it rises to the shoulder below the imposing rocky bastion of Castle Crag. Just left of the path, at its highest point, there is a curious pile of stones known as the 'Packhorseman's Grave'.

Stone avenue at foot of Riggindale

▶ Ascent of Castle Crag reveals ancient fortifications and a tremendous view down the length of Haweswater. It is however a strenuous climb. From the shoulder descend the path and keep along until it reaches the corner of a stone wall with large sycamores on the far side. From here

Over Haweswater to Riggindale

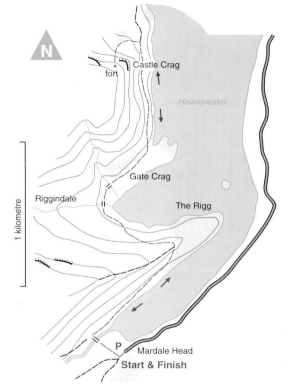

Castle Crag above Haweswater

branch off leftwards and steeply climb the fellside until easier going leads off left to the head of a little walled plantation.

▶ Above the trees a little grassy path zigzags steeply up the broad grassy gully to the right of Castle Crag. At the top of the gully go left, crossing two manmade defensive rock channels and climb the little pile of stone earthworks to top the ancient fort of Castle Crag. A commanding viewpoint looking over the entire length of the valley. Note: steep, unprotected crags lay beneath and descent must be made by exactly the same route.

Bridge over Randale Beck

WALK 80 FACT FILE

LENGTH: 6.5KM

TIME: 2 HOURS

DIFFICULTY: DIFFICULT; INCLUDING AN ASCENT OF CASTLE CRAG — EASY WITHOUT

START & FINISH: MARDALE HEAD CAR PARK AT HEAD OF HAWESWATER (469 107)

MAPS: OS L90 OR OL5

ACCESS: FROM PENRITH GO S ALONG THE A6 TO SHAP. FROM HERE A MINOR ROAD LEADS TO BAMPTON AND CONTINUES TO FOLLOW HAWESWATER

WATERING HOLES: NONE EN ROUTE;

HAWESWATER HOTEL ABOVE RESERVOIR AND ST PATRICK'S WELL INN AT BAMPTON NEARBY

▲CKNOWLEDGEMENTS

▲CKNOWLEDGEMENTS

I've long wanted to write and photograph this guidebook and many elements have finally come together to make it possible. I would personally like to thank the team at David & Charles, particularly Sue Viccars who brought the concept to fruition and art editor Sue Cleave who turned my requirements into practicable reality.

Similarly thanks must go to Martin Bagness, of Orienteering Services, whose knowledge of the complex terrain and ability to rationalise it into an attractive and straightforward map are, I believe, unsurpassed.

For accompanying me on many a walk, and locating themselves strategically as required, a special thanks to my family: my wife and first-draft editor, Susan, my daughter Rowan and my son William.

I am indebted to a great number of people for assisting me in this project, including those that walked the walks with me, became a part of my photographic imagery, shared their knowledge, corrected text and supported me personally:

Dave Birkett, Marian and Peter Cheung, Ann and Jackson Corrie, Brian and June Dodson, John Hargreaves, Alan Hinkes, Outdoor Writers Guild, Jon Rigby, Jenny Siddall, Andrew and Eszter Sheehan, Kyla Spady, Jo Squires, John and Gill White. For local knowledge and pronunciation thanks to Andrew, Ed, George, John, and Maureen Birkett, Melly and Marie Dixon, Jackie and Mark Dugdale. There were many more and I must offer my sincere apologies to those whose names I have missed.

Credit must also be given to those who keep a watchful eye over the Lake District and do a tremendous job preserving its beauty and character: the Lake District National Park Authority, the National Trust, the volunteers who selflessly do much good work to assist both bodies, the Countryside Commission, the Friends of the Lake District, and the various National Nature Reserves; also to those who have the best interests of the hill walker and mountaineer at heart – the Ramblers' Association, the British Mountaineering Council, the Open Spaces Society, the Climbers' Club and the Fell & Rock Climbing Club. A great deal of appreciation too, must be extended to those conscientious hill farmers who really know and love the land under their tenure and respect it accordingly.

For those who have helped to supply me with equipment a huge thanks to Sue Reay and Martin Geere of Berghaus – whose superb and constantly reliable gear, particularly boots and waterproofs, has kept me unfailingly walking and climbing in all types of extreme conditions. Also thanks to Dave Brown of DB Mountain Sports and Edelrid.

Bill Birkett Photo Library

All the photographs are my own, from the Bill Birkett Photo Library, and are 35mm colour transparencies. Researchers please note that the library holds a huge selection of material covering all of Britain's mountains and wild places, and is one of the most comprehensive available on the English Lake District.
Tel: 015594 37420.
E-mail: billbirkett@msn.com

A selection of Berghaus walking equipment

INDEX